Mastering

Electronic Dance Music

Mastering Electronic Dance Music is a guide to the sonic considerations of EDM audio. Written by a successful Apple-approved mastering engineer, it introduces readers to all the techniques behind mastering electronic dance music (EDM).

Beginning with the essentials of preparation, the book addresses the nature of mastering and the importance of listening. The chapters cover a wide range of topics including compression, EQ, saturation, metering, LUFS, and delivery formats. The book discusses all the processors involved in a mastering chain, finishing with a step-by-step guide of how they can be used, through an example of how a track by DJ Nicky Holloway was mastered. Covering plug-ins and hardware, this is an invaluable guide to mastering EDM, supported by numerous online audio examples.

This is an essential reference for anyone interested in producing or mastering EDM music, offering insights for beginners taking their first steps in engineering, as well as adept producers exploring new genres, and students of music production.

Alexandra Bartles is a UK Apple-approved mastering engineer specialising in electronic dance music who owns Altar Academy Studios, a studio dedicated to production, mixing, mastering, and training. She has mastered albums and singles for many artists, including Nicky Holloway, and is a member of the AES UK Executive Committee. Alex has collaborated with producers, writing melodies/lyrics for Warner, Mammas Milk, and 1980 Recordings.

Mastering
Electronic
Dance Music

An Essential Guide for EDM Producers

Alexandra Bartles

Routledge
Taylor & Francis Group

LONDON AND NEW YORK

Designed cover image: Alexandra Bartles

First published 2025
by Routledge
4 Park Square, Milton Park, Abingdon, Oxon OX14 4RN

and by Routledge
605 Third Avenue, New York, NY 10158

Routledge is an imprint of the Taylor & Francis Group, an informa business

© 2025 Alexandra Bartles

British Library Cataloguing-in-Publication Data
A catalogue record for this book is available from the British Library

Library of Congress Cataloging-in-Publication Data
Names: Bartles, Alexandra, author.
Title: Mastering electronic dance music : an essential guide for EDM producers / Alexandra Bartles.
Description: Abingdon, Oxon ; New York, NY : Routledge, 2025. |
Includes bibliographical references and index.
Identifiers: LCCN 2024037000 (print) | LCCN 2024037001 (ebook) |
ISBN 9781032685243 (hardback) | ISBN 9781032685199 (paperback) |
ISBN 9781032685229 (ebook)
Subjects: LCSH: Electronic dance music--Production and direction. | Sound recordings--Production and direction. | Mastering (Sound recordings)
Classification: LCC ML3540.5 .B37 2025 (print) | LCC ML3540.5 (ebook) |
DDC 781.648--dc23/eng/20240815
LC record available at https://lccn.loc.gov/2024037000
LC ebook record available at https://lccn.loc.gov/2024037001

ISBN: 978-1-032-68524-3 (hbk)
ISBN: 978-1-032-68519-9 (pbk)
ISBN: 978-1-032-68522-9 (ebk)

DOI: 10.4324/9781032685229

Typeset in Helvetica
by SPi Technologies India Pvt Ltd (Straive)

Access the Support Material: www.altaracademy.com

This is dedicated to the people who believe in me. Thank you for giving me the courage to follow my dream. This book is my way of showing you I was worth believing in.

Contents

Acknowledgements

Contrary to popular belief, we rarely do achieve anything alone. Unless we live in a bubble, we have been inspired, encouraged, taught, loved, and changed by those we meet. So, although my name is on the front of this book, I want to thank and acknowledge all the people who have encouraged me throughout my life.

The following people I have named because they have played a significant role in my music journey:

My family-thank you for believing in me and encouraging me in this wild endeavour:
    my Mum and Dad (Carol and Derek Bartles) and
    my dear brother Spud (Gary Bartles).
My close friends, Tracy Warburton and Denise Halliday.
Rick Snoman-for being patient and teaching an old dog new tricks. You helped open up a world I never dreamt I could be part of. With your encouragement and teaching, I have found my happy place. For this, I will be forever grateful and strive to further my knowledge so I can beat you at a game of pool and teach you the odd thing in music production.
Nicky Holloway-for allowing me to use his music as an example.
My amazing music friends, who I have the pleasure of working with and learning from. There are too many to name individually, but you know who you are so write your name here:

And yes, you must all buy a copy of this book, as you are now immortalised in print.

Introduction

I have been fortunate to work as a mastering engineer in this field for several years now, and during that time, I have had the opportunity to master music from various EDM producers, engineers, and labels. Some are famous with years of experience under their belts, and others are novices, but regardless of their skills, whenever I sit down at my desk with a track to master, I feel privileged to work with their music.

Every time, I learn a little more and develop my craft. Every day is a school day.

When I think back to when I first started to learn how to master, I was fortunate enough to train under a mentor with a well-respected background in the EDM community. Yet, I know that only some have this opportunity, and many have to learn from the limited material online.

There is plenty of advice for mastering pop, rock, classical, and jazz, but little anywhere relates to EDM. The books discussing it are self-published, with no peer review, and in my experience, contain inaccuracies and often some poor guesswork. Others talk about an unrelated genre and then, as a side comment, say you can also treat EDM the same.

I find this frustrating and disrespectful to any form of electronic dance music. I've grown tired of presenters demonstrating poor techniques, journalists and bloggers writing articles containing only half the facts, and readers being filled with misguided dogmas. Much of it is little more than graffiti with punctuation. It can sometimes feel like trying to learn a profession in the Wild West.

Furthermore, despite its popularity, many professionals still consider producing, mixing, or mastering EDM to require little to no talent.

DOI: 10.4324/9781032685229-1

Yet this couldn't be further from the truth. It varies from highly melodic to almost monotonic, encompassing a wide variety of subgenres, and has a diverse, educated, and demanding audience that knows what they want from the music.

In light of this, I wanted to offer a concise manual explaining how professional mastering engineers approach EDM. Although it could be argued that the approach is similar to mastering many other genres, there are many subtle (and not-so-subtle) differences when approaching electronic dance music.

To write this book, I start by describing what mastering involves before introducing the reader to the various processors we use to accomplish it. By discussing their functions and how they operate, we can discuss how a mastering engineer uses them to master a record. Then, when we understand our tools well, we can examine how we would tie all these processors together to produce the final master. This is the type of book I wish I had access to when first starting my journey as a mastering engineer.

However, reading or glancing over this book will not transform you into a world-class mastering engineer. Mastering is a profession and an art form, requiring research, repetition, and, most importantly, practice. It is not a prefix chain of processors; we must understand each one and consider whether they are required for each specific piece of music.

Furthermore, while we cannot practice mastering while travelling to work, if you have 5 minutes to spare, put your phone and social media down and pick up a manual or this book. Read them repeatedly because this is how you build a living and growing map of knowledge and inspiration.

All manuals are inspiring documents that challenge you to try techniques and listen to the results. Remember, you are learning how to master music, not how your mobile phone works. Bringing all these nuggets of information from manuals, experimentation, listening, and practice will enable you to develop a mature and professional mastery approach.

This is the first edition of the EDM Mastering Manual, and as techniques, music, and technology change, I plan to adapt to it with further editions. If you have any suggestions for inclusions in the next edition, I'm not unavailable, and I appreciate your input. You can contact me at www.altaracademy.com.

Finally, I would like to thank Nicky Holloway for allowing me to use one of his tracks as an example for this book. We've been mastering his work at Altar for several years, and the opportunity to use the music of one of the original DJs who brought house music to the United Kingdom feels fitting for a book on how to master EDM.

Chapter 1
What Is Mastering

Many opinions, definitions, and practices exist when discussing mastering. They range from the process amounting to little more than making the music as loud as absolutely possible via limiting or aiming for a specific loudness similar to other songs. It can sometimes be about obtaining a second opinion or employing one of the many online artificial intelligence (AI) mastering services.

Confusion is certainly nothing new in the music production industry, whether in terminology or techniques. Much of it stems from the fast-paced industry developments over the last 30 years. However, much of this confusion can also be accredited to the cheap availability of the tools required to master a record.

Initially, mastering required a sizeable physical studio, a substantial monetary investment, and years of training. In many situations, engineers would work up the "ladder" to become mastering engineers, bringing all their knowledge with them.

However, today, anyone with a reasonably priced laptop and access to the internet can have a working mastering studio at their fingertips. Indeed, if the internet is to be believed, you can produce and master an international hit with little more than a laptop and a few well-kept secrets. The problem, however, is that many new to mastering procedures lack the necessary training and often require clarification about what mastering really entails and its main purpose.

Indeed, many online articles and videos are misguided, and this misinformation spreads like wildfire as it is copied and regurgitated over many more websites and videos, further confusing the process. So, for

DOI: 10.4324/9781032685229-2

the first chapter of this book, we should first clarify what mastering is, where it came from, and why it is so vital.

Mastering engineers first appeared in the 1940s when tape machines were introduced into the recording process. The audio material recorded onto the magnetic tape had to be transferred to vinyl, requiring "Transfer Engineers". This is because magnetic tape had a much more extensive dynamic range than vinyl, which has several limitations inherent to its design.

Vinyl is unsuited for storing bass frequencies because low frequencies require much wider grooves than higher frequencies. The lower the frequency, the wider the vinyl groove must become to accommodate it. Indeed, the higher the frequency, the less the needle needs to modulate (move left and right) to reproduce it. Therefore, fitting many tracks onto a vinyl record is difficult if they all exhibit excessive low-frequency bass.

Phase can also cause problems with vinyl; while it can be easily recorded on a magnetic medium such as tape, any severe phase discrepancies in the music will result in the needle jumping out of the groove. Moreover, the needle on a vinyl player is highly sensitive, and the smallest dust particles will create pops, clicks, and crackles. These sudden bursts of energy could be loud enough to damage speakers.

To address these, the transfer engineers employed filters, commonly 6 dB per octave, to gradually reduce the amplitude of low frequencies in the music while amplifying the high frequencies. By doing so, as the frequency became lower, it would exhibit less amplitude; as the frequency increased, it would increase in amplitude.

Of course, this meant that listening back to any track mastered for vinyl would be devoid of bass and exhibit excessively high frequencies, making the music unlistenable. Consequently, the amplifier attached to the vinyl player would artificially increase the lows and reduce the highs on playback, returning the music to its original levels.

This approach permitted the label to fit more tracks onto a vinyl record while ensuring that any pops or crackles resulting from dust on the record would not damage the speaker. The pre-EQ performed by the transfer engineer and the post-EQ performed by the amplifier are known as pre- and de-emphasis.

Throughout the 1940s, there was no standardisation for these emphasis procedures, and therefore, music would sound different depending on the engineer and the amplifier. In 1954, the Recording Industry Association of America (RIAA) introduced the RIAA equalisation curve, which became an internationally adopted standard. This meant that regardless of the engineer, the playback quality would be similar to other records. I say similar, because the authentic sound of vinyl that everyone loves is not so much a result of the vinyl as it is the de-emphasis performed by the amplifier during playback (Figure 1.1).

Despite this equalisation curve, however, low frequencies still require a wider groove on vinyl. Therefore, many mastering engineers would also determine the order of the tracks on an album. Placing bass-heavy tracks near the beginning was essential as there is less room towards the centre of the record. Furthermore, as recording and studio techniques developed and changed over the years, and music tracks were recorded over months, each often mixed at different times by different engineers; the mastering engineer also had to ensure that each track matched in both volume and dynamics so there were no sudden surprises when listening to the album.

The release of Compact Disc in 1983 changed the goal of mastering. Engineers no longer had to follow the RIAA equalisation curve, as CD exhibited a far higher dynamic range, and there were no limitations on lower frequencies. Plus, as dust made no difference, there was no

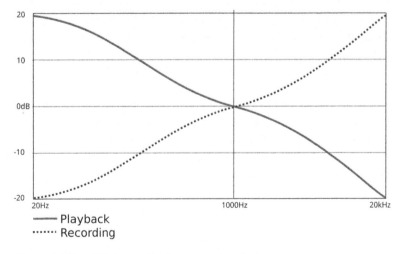

Figure 1.1 The RIAA equalisation curve for vinyl.

requirement to increase the higher frequencies artificially, and phase issues were no longer a problem. However, this freedom from constraints also had a negative effect.

Louder always sounds invariably better to the human ear, so the louder the music, the more we tend to appreciate it. With the dynamic limitations of vinyl removed, engineers would now push their limiters to the extreme, clipping converters to heavily restrict the dynamics of the music and produce the loudest music possible on the format. This initiated the loudness wars that, although showing some signs of abating, are still occurring, particularly with electronic dance music (EDM). The producers of these genres feel their music should be loud because that's how they experience it in a club environment. I'll challenge this common misconception throughout the book.

Today, with streaming services, albums are less popular than they once were, and many artists will release individual songs, so there is no longer a requirement to ensure consistency throughout an album. Indeed, EDM producers, in particular, release separate tracks without the intention of ever producing an album.

Consequently, many believe the only purpose of mastering is to make a song as loud as possible with a limiter. Yet, in reality, a mastering engineer's job has become more multifaceted with new technology, not less.

Despite rumours abounding the internet, mastering cannot fix a poor mix; it isn't magical wizardry or smoke and mirrors, nor is it just applying excessive limiting to increase the overall amplitude of a track. While part of the purpose is to increase the overall amplitude of a mix, it also involves preparing the music for playback on multiple systems, ensuring it sounds appropriate on *all* devices, not just club systems. It should also sound great on headphones, home systems and even smart speakers.

This necessitates more than limiting the music to gain higher amplitudes, it may require EQ, dynamic manipulation, stereo control or widening, mono compatibility, saturation, clipping, and various other techniques to ensure it sounds the best it possibly can. Then again, it may require nothing more than limiting.

Listening to a piece of music and determining whether it requires processing is one of the most significant skills of any mastering engineer. There have been occasions where I've had to do little more than apply some gentle limiting, but others where I have spent a day correcting any number of problems. It all depends on the music; no fixed process or chain of processors will work for all music. It requires you to listen to the music and make educated judgements on what would benefit the music.

One thing is for sure: unnecessary application of processing or effects will irreparably harm a track. Mastering requires both technical and scientific knowledge and the application of specific techniques. We need an understanding of industry and streaming standards, an idea of where you aim to have the track played, the ability to listen with intent, and the ability to be creative with all these constraints.

However, the most important thing to note when mastering music is that no industry standards exist. While many websites promise to master to some mysterious, unnamed industry standard, it's meaningless and bears no weight. Sure, radio and TV require some standards to be adhered to for broadcast, but there are no hard and fast rules for streaming; it's little more than marketing talk to give you confidence in them as a service provider.

However, this should not grant you a license to do whatever you want. As you'll discover throughout this book, while there may be no ideal standards, we should work to some standard to ensure our music sounds the best it possibly can.

Chapter 2
Mastering Options

As discussed in the previous chapter, all music requires mastering regardless of the playback medium. As many electronic dance musicians do not release albums or release on vinyl, mastering this genre is not about ensuring continuity between different records but ensuring the track will translate accurately on as many speaker systems as possible.

This is more difficult than it may first appear because many tutorials can be misleading. It is not solely about placing a limiter on the stereo bus and setting it to stun or aiming to make it as loud as your favourite record of the month. If it were, there would be no need for this book, mastering engineers or artificial intelligence (AI) mastering. We could all purchase a limiter and just use it to increase the amplitude of the medium. However, before examining the intricacies and processing involved in mastering electronic dance music, we should assess the options available and discuss the pros and cons. We can start with AI mastering, as many websites offer this service.

Artificial Intelligence

With AI mastering, you upload your track to the service, pay a fee, and inform the "AI" what style of music it is. The track is then "mastered", and you can download your finalised mastered version within a few minutes. While this may seem like the perfect solution, from my experience, it isn't, and I've managed to fool them several times over.

DOI: 10.4324/9781032685229-3

First, AI is a misnomer because it cannot perform tasks outside a predetermined set of parameters. Instead, it's a buzzword that sells an idea more appealable than simply imprinting an equalisation (EQ) curve and loudness onto the music. Indeed, Sterne and Razlogova challenge the idea of whether these services are based on AI at all in a paper available online at https://journals.sagepub.com/doi/10.1177/2056305 119847525.

In this paper, they argue that online services such as LANDR offer clients only three "intensities" for their music, which shows a lack of intelligence in the system. In contrast, a mastering engineer will make many microscopic choices and adjustments. Furthermore, while LANDR suggests they use machine learning, it likely only plays a minimal role in the application.

Similarly, all-in-one mastering software such as Ozone is described as using machine learning. Yet, at a presentation at NAMM 2019, the presenter conceded that it performs no such function when processing audio on a user's computer; it was only employed during the application's design.

To quote Sterne and Razlogova directly, "LANDR also clearly plays on this ambiguity: AI becomes synecdochic for everything the software does, and in so doing, works more like a marketing term than an explanation of anything."

AI cannot think independently nor understand emotion or the nuances of human behaviour or creativity. Indeed, John Searles's thought experiment can explain the actual behaviour of AI. In this thought experiment, you imagine yourself locked in a room surrounded by baskets, each filled with Chinese characters. While you cannot speak the language, you have a rule book stating that if you see symbol A, you must reply with symbol X, etc.

If someone outside the room were to slip symbols underneath the door to you, using the rule book, you could reply to each symbol. The person on the other side of the door would believe you are fluent in the language. In reality, however, you cannot assign any meaning to them; you're simply following a predetermined set of instructions.

When you submit your music to AI, it cannot assign any meaning to your music. Instead, it will use a series of algorithms to measure the tonal balance and volume of the music and then apply a series of processors to produce an average against other preselected targets.

However, while it's easy to measure integrated loudness and the spectral composition of music, the preselected targets it measures against must be similar, and this is where things often go awry.

Mastering is more than the sum of its tools; most producers can use the stock limiters, compression and EQs in a Digital Audio Workstation (DAW) to copy the tonal balance from another song or make it louder, but experienced engineers are more than a series of plug-ins; they are also artists.

They know how to apply EQ, compression, saturation, and limiting to provide warmth, consistency, energy, and vibe to help connect the song with its listeners. Mastering, like mixing and production, is an art form; they do not win Grammys for simply "turning the music up" or copying the tonal balance from another record.

Furthermore, AI mastering cannot discern errors like crackles, clicks, pops, and noise. Moreover, as it occurs entirely in the digital domain, it risks introducing aliasing into the signal (more on this later).

Perhaps more importantly, the system can be fooled. I tested a popular online mastering service by uploading a liquid drum and bass track that began with a soft orchestral string section before dropping into heavy-hitting drum and bass after a minute.

The returned master was lacking. I suspect this resulted from the system attempting to reach a specific LUFS value (a volume averaged across the entire piece of music) while equally becoming confused over what preselected target it should match. A human engineer would have approached it more thoughtfully, dealing with the more dynamic orchestral introduction differently than the hard-hitting beats during the drop.

Notably, this automated mastering process has begun to creep into the DAW environment; Logic Pro (a DAW we use in the studio) has introduced a mastering plug-in. You inform the plug-in what algorithm it should use, and it masters the track on your behalf.

While I typically use Steinberg Wavelab to master music, I've tried Logic's mastering plugin numerous times, and the results were questionable. In many instances, the mastering EQ created strange mid-range increases that were not suited to the material, and often, it would exceed the specified amplitude and LUFS values.

I'm not suggesting these automated mastering services are useless. They can be used as a rough idea to send to friends for their opinions or employed as a training tool. I'm also not a second-generation Luddite. I use technology daily and welcome technological advancements, but from my professional experience, AI should perform mundane tasks such as answering emails, not mastering music or acting in any creative manner.

While some argue that it offers an alternative, allowing people who currently can't receive quality mastering to have an opportunity to do so, I disagree. Professional mastering is not expensive, and the "democratisation of music" has only doubled our work to pay a fraction of what we used to receive.

Indeed, this democratisation we "all wanted" has resulted in over 1.2 million records uploaded to streaming services every month. According to the Luminates Year End Music Report 2024, 158.6 million tracks on Spotify have fewer than 1,000 plays, and therefore, the royalties are shared among those with more plays, so you receive nothing. Moreover, nearly a quarter of songs, 24.8%, have zero plays.

Professional mastering is not prohibitively expensive, and professionals who value their music pay professionals to work on it. It's only when we place no value on our music that we do not value any other process in the chain.

If you want to avoid paying a professional, then rather than use AI mastering, I recommend you perform the mastering yourself. While it is only 1 to 3% of the production process, what you perform here has massive implications. To perform the master, you will require the following skills:

1.   The gear and knowledge of how to use it.
2.   Developed listening skills
3.   Several techniques.

This book will give you a good grounding on the tools and the techniques, but listening skills come with practice. Furthermore, while you may understand the theory and principles behind mastering, experience is the true teacher.

Mastering is like any other art form and requires consistent practice before becoming good at it. The first time you master a track, it won't be that impressive, but if you implement the guidance in this book, you will build your skills. I practised a great deal, and to support that practice,

I had a mentor. A mentor or coach will guide you through your skill development as you gain experience. However, you must ensure you gain the right experience; repeating something ad nauseam does not mean what you practice is right.

The "10,000-hour rule", popularised by author Malcolm Gladwell, is often referred to when gaining experience. This rule, from his book *Outliers: The Story of Success*, states that to become an expert at a skill, we must repeat it for at least 10,000 hours. This theory has a significant flaw, though; if what we are repeating is incorrect, then we just become good at being bad.

To gain good experience, you must be trained correctly. This means acquiring the correct theory, followed by practical application. How do you know you correctly executed the practical application when working alone?

We only have to consider an athlete who wants to qualify to win an Olympic gold medal in hurdles. They will know how to run and jump a hurdle, but then they must implement that theory on the racetrack. A successful athlete will train with a coach.

I recommend a mentor who is practically experienced and knowledgeable about the theory. Some factors to consider when selecting a mentor:

1.   Their experience
2.   Can you approach them?

When considering their experience, selecting a mentor you aspire to be is always worth it. They might have won awards in mastering, worked with artists you admire, or worked in a place you want to work in.

I strongly recommend against asking a peer to review your work. Many individuals suffer from the Dunning-Kruger Effect, a cognitive bias that results in individuals demonstrating overconfidence in a skill with limited competence. In other words, a peer might appear competent, but they may just be confident.

I witnessed this on Soundcloud when a client sent me a link to their latest track and all their other production peers. They asked for feedback on the production, and most of the feedback received was positive, despite it being poorly produced and mixed, only demonstrating further that the peers didn't know what they were listening for either.

If you're all in the ocean together and nobody knows how to swim, you'll drown together. Mind you, there will always be that one person who takes their pants off, ties knots, and inflates them for a flotation device. However, while this quick fix might work in the ocean, it will not work in mastering; there are no quick fixes in music.

I recommend keeping a detailed notebook to record what you learn from manuals, articles or books. Then, practice the techniques and review them, if possible, with your mentor. If you don't have a mentor, reflect on the outcomes yourself. Much of what we do in audio relies on us being able to react fast before our ears suffer from any form of fatigue. If you develop the habit of reflection after completing a process, you will remember actions and audio outcomes. This will be beneficial as you progress and grow, as you will work faster and more accurately.

Chapter 3
Monitoring for Mastering

I suspect many reading this will be music producers looking to master their own music. Therefore, I assume you will already have a monitoring set up. In many smaller home studios, this often consists of an interface and a pair of headphones, but you will also require speaker monitors for mastering. Indeed, your monitoring system is one of the most essential tools you have; if you can't hear it, you can't work with it.

While a studio's audio monitoring system isn't exactly a sexy topic, or at least not as sexy as a piece of hardware that illuminates blue or has tubes that glow, it is nonetheless essential. A monitoring set-up can start at a bundle price of approximately £300 (consumer level) to more than £20,000 (pro status).

Although some journalists and presenters in the media argue that you don't need to invest in this part of the studio because you can trust an "FFT" to tell you what the monitors can't, that's not exactly true. Fast Fourier Transform (FFT) metering becomes inaccurate once you reach below approximately 100 Hz for reasons that will be discussed later.

If you look at any successful professional studio, they have invested heavily in their monitoring system; this alone should indicate their importance. Indeed, like production, investing as much as possible in your equipment is essential, as this is the final stage the track goes through before it's exposed to the public.

If your monitors aren't up to the job, you must constantly test your masters on as many different systems as possible alongside your car to check it sounds right, which can be time-consuming. It will also become annoying when you reach *finalfinalfinaldefinitelyFINALmaster16.wav*.

We've all been there. If you haven't yet, you will.

DOI: 10.4324/9781032685229-4

For mastering, we must accept that all set-ups have limitations unless you spend a substantial amount of money. This may not necessarily be your speakers but the audio interface or the room. You can perform mastering with a pro-consumer-level set-up, but you need to know and understand the limitations of these setups and the advantages a pro-level system will provide.

First, we should consider the audio interface.

When selecting your audio interface for production, you will likely have considered factors such as connectivity to the DAW (USB or Thunderbolt) and connections for speakers/monitors, headphones, and hardware (1/4" (6.35 mm) jack sockets and XLR connections).

Interfaces for mastering are less about connectivity and more focused on sound quality. Indeed, many mastering interfaces will feature only a couple of XLR connections for inputs and outputs and little else! (Figure 3.1)

I use a different audio interface for mastering than the one used for production and mixing in the studio because I need to hear the highest

Figure 3.1 Lynx Hilo Mastering Converter.

audio quality with the lowest levels of distortion and noise. If your audio interface is cheap, I advise investing in something more substantial for mastering. Sub £300 interfaces exhibit a higher distortion, particularly on lower frequencies. Furthermore, the system's frequency response can often be uneven, and the A/D D/A conversion quality is commonly low, resulting in a restricted soundstage. These are all essential features you must take into account.

If you plan on mastering everything in the box, only the D/A converters are essential, but if you plan on using hardware, you must ensure that both D/A and A/D are of good quality. Moreover, the headphone amplifiers in many audio interfaces often leave a little to be desired, so if you plan to master entirely on headphones, you must use high-quality headphones and amplifiers or ensure your audio interface amplifier is up to the job. Indeed, if you plan on using headphones with your audio interface, you must ensure they have a "matched" impedance.

Impedance describes a form of electrical resistance; all audio equipment will experience this because all materials resist the flow of electrons. There is more to impedance, but it's a subject that requires further electrical knowledge, which is beyond the scope of this book.

Impedance is measured in Ohms and generally speaking, the higher the headphones' impedance, the better their sound quality. This is because further windings on the voice coil will produce a more refined sonic result but will equally exhibit a higher impedance value, requiring more voltage to "move" the headphone drivers.

To accomplish this, the audio interface or amplifier impedance must be less than an eighth of the headphones, a ratio known as a damping factor. If it isn't, you will likely be unable to listen at higher volumes when using your headphones, or they may suffer from low-level distortions.

You can determine the impedance required from your headphone amplifier or audio interface by dividing the headphone impedance by eight. For example, a popular impedance for quality headphones is 650 Ohm, so your interface should have an impedance of less than 80 Ohms (**650/8 = 81**).

However, we cannot *always* judge the quality of headphones by their impedance value alone. Some mastering headphones will use planar magnetic drivers. While these are expensive, they often exhibit an impedance as low as 14 Ohms and sometimes even less! (Figure 3.2).

Figure 3.2 Audeze LCD-5 headphones.

If you use these, you *will* require a specialised headphone amplifier because the output impedance of many audio interfaces is relatively high. For example, the SSL 2+ audio interfaces have a headphone output impedance of 10 Ohms, which would not suitably drive some planar magnet headphones, resulting in low amplitudes and low-level distortion artefacts.

I use a Little Labs "The Monitor" headphone amplifier because it has an ultra-low impedance of 0.5 Ohms and provides a sonically neutral response compared to most typical audio interface headphone amplifiers. This clarity is essential during mastering. The goal is to create a final track that is clear of any unwanted distortion, pops, or other artefacts that might be introduced at the production or mixing stage or via some mastering plug-ins. We must listen with the highest-quality monitoring system possible to identify those artefacts. (Figure 3.3).

Figure 3.3 The Little Labs monitor headphone amplifier.

Again, these specific headphone amplifiers are costly, but audio equipment should always be financially balanced. There is no point in spending thousands on headphones if the amplifier you connect to is only £200.

Of course, not everyone can afford to invest a few thousand pounds in a pair of planar magnetic headphones, but you should research what headphones are best for mastering duties within your allotted budget.

Research extends beyond asking someone on a forum and requires active participation. Almost every manufacturer has manuals available online, so you should read these, alongside reading reviews and searching for what other engineers use.

Some engineers prefer closed back, and some prefer open back. Some prefer a mix of both. Some don't like either. However, this research will allow you to make informed decisions, which is vital for your work.

I prefer to use open-back headphones for mastering. Closed-back are designed to create a seal around the ear, directing the sound directly into the ear canal. This design eliminates external noise and produces a quiet listening environment. These provide an excellent bass response, but because they clamp tightly on your head, the frequencies cannot escape anywhere, creating sonic reflections resulting in dips and peaks in the frequency spectrum. They also have a limited soundstage, making instrument placement challenging to decipher with any accuracy. Plus, they can be uncomfortable to wear for prolonged periods.

Open-back are more comfortable to wear, but more importantly, they permit frequencies to escape through a headphone cup grill. By avoiding creating a sealed environment, they produce a far better soundstage, which is closer to the experience of listening to monitors in a room. However, this comes at the expense of a more-defined bass frequency.

Investing in headphones that employ planar drivers is the only way to achieve everything reasonab*ly* reliably. I use Audeze (*pronounced Odyssey*) LCD-5 open-back planar headphones. These headphones have an impedance of 14 Ohms, matching the impedance of my headphone amplifier, which, as discussed, is rated at 0.5 Ohms. However, neither the headphone amplifier nor the headphones are what I would call cheap.

Regardless of your choice, it is essential to ensure they are positioned correctly on your head because the wrong size or poor misalignment can seriously affect the frequency response. When wearing them, you should always consider the following:

• Do they fit over the whole of my pinna (the cartilage part of the ear on the side of the head),?
• Does my hair prevent the headphone ear cushion from maintaining a good seal?
• Do I wear glasses, and do they prevent a good seal?
• Is the band the correct tension?
• Are the headphones too tight and crushing the ear?

Poor fit/placement can result in air leakage, resulting in a loss of bass below 50 Hz and a boost of as much as 15 dB at the midrange frequencies. Furthermore, if they are tight or heavy, they can cause the ear canal to collapse, affecting frequencies above 1 kHz.

Even if the headphones fit correctly, we should rely only partially on them during mastering. Our ears are positioned on opposite sides of our head, which means that depending on the location of the sound, our brain will allow for a time delay of sound reaching one ear before another or head shadow; this is referred to as interaural time difference (ITD) and head-related transfer function (HRTF).

Our pinna, ear canal, head, and body play an essential role in our perception and location of different frequencies and wearing head-phones changes all this. Of course, some software programs and hard-ware attempt to emulate these phenomena via a matrix that adjusts the timing differences between each cup in the headphone. These, how-ever, are hit-and-miss for many professionals because they rarely pro-vide truly accurate results comparable to monitors, and often, they can make you unwittingly introduce phase issues into the music.

Consequently, we should also reference mastering work on a good pair of monitors alongside headphones. Studio monitors we use for pro-duction and mastering must exhibit a neutral frequency response. They will often have deliberately induced dips in the midrange frequencies if they are not neutral.

Many consumer speakers are non-neutral to improve our listening experience. They are designed to create the smiley face EQ. This is signified by a dip in the midrange frequencies and a slight boost in the high and low frequencies. This form of EQ replicates the experience of listening to music at an increased volume because as amplitude increases, the midrange appears quieter while bass and high frequen-cies increase. If we use these speakers, we will over-compensate for that midrange dip, and the music will not be accurate on other systems.

However, although many studio monitors are designed to be neutral, not all are, no matter what manufacturers state. Budget studio monitors often do not have a neutral response and cannot accurately propagate all frequencies. Note that I said propagate, not reproduce. A common thread online is that smaller speaker systems cannot replicate bass frequencies. This is inaccurate; a well-designed speaker can reproduce *all* frequencies; otherwise, you would have no bass in your EarPods.

Instead, smaller speakers cannot move the air required to produce bass at higher amplitudes. Therefore, it is the distance between you and the speaker that matters. The smaller the speaker, the closer you must be to the speaker's driver to hear the lower frequencies. This is evident in the formula: *Energy/Time * Area = Sound Intensity*. Of course, if you have smaller monitors, it can be tempting to add a subwoofer to your set-up so that you can hear the bass, particularly if working with EDM, but I would recommend against it.

Subwoofers are designed to reproduce frequencies below approximately 120 Hz, while frequencies above this are delivered to speaker monitors, now known as satellites. To employ a subwoofer, the signal leaves your audio interface and enters the subwoofer, where the frequency is divided. Low frequencies are replicated via the subwoofer, and the rest of the signal is delivered to the monitors.

The problem with this approach is that if the frequency crossover is not properly aligned, it will introduce phase issues that amplify at the crossover point, often producing arbitrary unwanted boosts throughout the lower frequency range. Moreover, if it is placed at a different distance from you than your monitors, it will create further phasing issues. This is not to mention that accurately reproducing low frequencies is one of the most challenging things to ask of any speaker, and good-quality subwoofers require a large cone, a well-tuned cabinet, and an excellent linear amplifier.

Alongside an accurate bass representation, we must also consider the volume we listen to the music because this will affect the excursion period of the monitor drivers.

The kick is essential to electronic dance music; it should punch listeners in the chest and rattle their teeth. Indeed, we should never underestimate the feeling a kick provides listeners, particularly in a club environment. It is so essential that many producers spend a significant amount of their time creating kicks during production, and while mastering, we must always ensure we maintain this energy.

The excursion value determines the speaker drivers' maximum inward and outward movement (speaker cone). As volume increases, the driver will move further towards its limits. The punch of electronic dance music comes from how much louder the kick is (the peak value) from the body of the music (the Root Mean Square (RMS) value). If there is a significant peak-to-RMS ratio, the kick will punch hard because of a high dynamic difference between the kick and body of the music. If the peak-to-RMS is lower, the kick will be closer to the body of the music and the kick will not punch as much.

If we translate this action to the excursion value of monitors, if the driver has a maximum excursion of 6 mm, then listening at a low volume, the RMS value may move the cone by 4 mm. When the kick occurs, due to a higher peak-to-RMS ratio, the kick will move the cone out by a further 2 mm, producing an energetic thump to the music.

Suppose the monitoring volume is increased and the total movement of the cone (RMS and peak value added together) is >6 mm. In that case, distortion will occur at every peak because the speaker cannot exceed its excursion value. This distorts the representation of the signal, adding further harmonics, which can appear to improve the music – that is, until you listen to it on different speakers, and it sounds terrible.

We must also consider the driver's design. A speaker driver employs a copper winding called a coil. An electrical current travels along this coil, transferring energy to a magnet and forcing the speaker cone into motion. The coil's temperature will increase if you listen to your music close to the speaker's maximum efficiency, and as it does so, its resistance increases, diminishing the speaker's capability to reproduce the audio accurately.

Monitor Placement

The placement of the monitors and the surrounding area may also negatively impact the sound emanating from the drivers. Even the best, most expensive monitors in a room with a poor response will become useless. Although room acoustics and monitoring choice are complex fields that justify a lifetime of study dedicated to the topic, I can discuss the primary considerations you need to be aware of and consider.

Many home/semi-professional producers will likely use nearfield studio monitors. The usual advice is that you and the monitors should form an equilateral triangle; that is, if the monitors are 2 m apart, you should be sat 2 m away from them. However, this is rarely the case in practice because the room's dimensions also play a role.

Instead, it would be best if you sat in your listening position, listening to your favourite music. Place the monitors side by side, then have an assistant slowly move the monitors further apart. When you hear the stereo spectrum begin to lose coherence, stop and move them back towards the centre by 100 cm. This will provide a more accurate environment than following the equilateral triangle theory.

If the monitors are designed to stand vertically or horizontally, you must use them in that position. Flipping a monitor on its side is like flipping a gun on its side in gangster films; it looks cool, but it's inappropriate and not designed to be used that way. Positioning a monitor incorrectly can degrade the stereo image and the dispersion of the higher frequencies. Studio monitors are designed to be vertical, horizontal, or multi-placement.

When positioning the monitors, the ideal height is for the tweeters to sit at ear level, typically 1.2–1.4 meters from the floor. However, this depends on your chair, your height and your desk. If they must be placed higher due to constraints, they can be tilted down towards your ears, but this angle should not exceed more than 15 degrees; otherwise, it will affect the frequencies you hear.

Alongside the monitors, the room will also influence what you hear. When sound is created, it moves air, creating a sound wave that reflects off all the objects in your room, creating a series of standing waves. The longer the waveform (i.e., the lower the frequency), the more problematic these waves become. While I would like to advise that if you have the funds, you should employ a room acoustician to design your studio and repair these problems, this is often far from reality for many.

Therefore, the simplest solution to rectifying some of the problems experienced with these waves is to open a window or a door. Still, alongside this, I recommend using room correction software. Several developers now sell software with a microphone; you install the software, and the monitors produce a series of test tones. You move around the room with the microphone until it measures the room, and then the software corrects the standing waves and modal problems using an EQ.

While this isn't as efficient as having the room designed specifically for you, it is a much cheaper alternative and will, at the very least, give you a good approximation of how the music sounds.

Chapter 4
The Tools for Mastering

Today, when it comes to studios, we're privileged. What would have initially cost thousands to build and develop can now be carried around in a laptop for very little investment. Only 40 years ago, we would need to invest thousands in hardware, whereas today, you can have emulations for significantly less. However, while this is advantageous to many, the easy availability of the tools also has its downside.

Even though we have access to the tools, we still need to become adept at using them. My dog has constant access to my studio, but I'm not sure she can use any equipment. Many producers believe they must be world-class mixing and mastering engineers because they can access the same tools. This is not the case, as mastering and production are a profession. While some may scoff, it is no different from a brain surgeon, accountant, or builder; we have learnt our trade over many years.

Owning a laptop crammed with plugins is just one of the many things you will need to master music; for example, developing listening skills and knowing your tools is essential. Both the software and hardware you decide to use should be appropriate for what you want to accomplish. Just as you wouldn't use a hammer as a screwdriver, you shouldn't use the wrong processors for mastering music.

Of course, whenever hardware and software are discussed in the same sentence, there is usually a heated discussion about whether software is as good as hardware. Yet, there is no argument; you should choose the best tool for the job, regardless of its origin.

Indeed, you should know what you want to achieve and research the appropriate tools to accomplish it. I would expect a surgeon to know

DOI: 10.4324/9781032685229-5

that a craft knife is not the tool for the job when making an incision for a heart transplant.

Hardware will sometimes be better than software in some instances, and software will be better than hardware in others. This is why, if you examine any professional mastering studio, you will see a mix of hardware and software.

Notably, producers and mastering engineers are not the only ones concerned about whether hardware or digital software is used in music. It appears that some of the listening public are, too. Upon the release of CDs and digital media, many listeners wanted to know whether their favourite albums were recorded, mixed, and mastered through analogue or digital gear. To address this, the Society of Professional Audio Recording Services (SPARS) created a classification system to inform listeners.

They did this using a code with "A" for analogue and "D" for digital, displayed on the CD cover art. The first letter refers to the method used in the initial audio recording, the second for mixing, and the third for mastering.

An example of SPARS:
> **AAD**: Analogue recording, Analogue Mixing, Digital Mastering.
> **DAD**: Digital recording, Analogue Mixing, Digital Mastering.

This method was used until the mid-to-late 1990s when MP3 media players began to reach the markets. Fewer seemed to care whether software or hardware was used in the recording, production, or mastering process. This is likely due to the MP3 media itself being a compressed format.

While the public has less of an interest as to whether their music is mastered via digital or analogue means, it does remain an important consideration to many professional mastering engineers. For example, saturation and EQ in the box can result in aliasing frequencies that molest the program material, adding unwanted harmonics that negatively affect the media. Therefore, hardware will be the preferred option for some processing, whereas performing small surgical frequency adjustments is often better accomplished in software.

Most professionals, including myself, use a mix of both; dynamic compression in hardware tends to sound better than in software because it opens the soundstage and doesn't damage the spectra, whereas digital compression tends to reduce the soundstage and add side band harmonics that may damage the program material. Depending on the job, I use a mix of digital and hardware for EQ. When limiting, I will use analogue limiting but then add a final, small application of limiting in the digital realm. This provides the best of both worlds and if you want to master your music professionally, I recommend this approach rather than just one or the other.

Indeed, a good mastering studio should consist of hardware and software. From personal experience, dynamics, saturation, and wideband EQ perform better in hardware due to the lack of aliasing, frequency cramping, and problems with coding dynamic restriction while maintaining a soundstage. However, the software performs better for surgical adjustments and look-ahead processing.

Of course, mastering hardware is expensive, but it is no different than purchasing monitors; you get what you pay for, and you can spend a relatively small amount or a considerable amount of money. For example, one of my mastering compressors cost a little over £4,500, and one of the limiters was over £5,000. While these are substantial outlays, and you can buy software replicas for £39.95, the manufacturers are either committing financial suicide, or there is a significant difference in the quality between the two.

This is not to suggest that you cannot produce a successful master using only software; rather, the final results will be unable to compete against an experienced professional using a hybrid setup (Figure 4.1).

Figure 4.1 My SPL Iron mastering compressor hardware. The plugin looks the same, but it doesn't sound the same.

Mastering hardware is expensive because it must retain the signal's integrity while performing with minimal unwanted artefacts. The topology to accomplish this is not cheap. Furthermore, the switches and rotary dials on mastering equipment are usually stepped so you can recall if required, and quality stepped rotary dials are expensive to implement.

Most mastering hardware switches and rotary controls will be either stepped, discrete detented, free-flow detented or discrete. I've noted over the years that manufacturers tend to interchange these terms when describing their products, so much so that it can become confusing, especially if you are new to hardware. Therefore, the following are the definitions of each style.

A. **Stepped Rotary Control**

This clicks at each turn. It is a linear progressive parameter. For example, if used for gain, it will give an impression of a linear sound increase.

B. **Discrete Detented Rotary Control**

Discrete is a term used to explain opposing effects, such as on or off. A discrete dented rotary control will have several options/functions/ parameters, and the controller will turn them on or off. You select Off, EQ1, EQ2, on the SPL Iron.

C. **Free-Flow Detented Rotary Control**

This rotary control will stop at specific points. The most typical application is a volume parameter on an EQ; it will move freely in positive or negative, but the centre (zero) position is detented to inform you that no processing is taking place.

D. **Discrete Switch**

This is a two-way switch that is either on or off. They are typically bypass, power, or activation switches.

Most mastering hardware will be detended and stepped on all rotary encoders. This ensures that if the hardware is dual-mono, you can configure both sides to be the same, but it also helps with recall.

Recall is essential for mastering; we're all fallible, and because mastering usually consists of minimal movements, we can sometimes miss something that only becomes evident when we hear it in another context. With stepped controllers, we can make notes of the settings and recall them later with high accuracy. Alongside documenting the settings, I also take photographs of the hardware settings and store them in a file until the label approves the master.

Of course, this recall isn't a problem with software because all the settings are saved with the original project file. Some hardware is hybrid, however, and will store the settings from the hardware digitally in the DAW so they are recalled when the project is opened. The BetterMaker mastering limiter is an example of one such device.

Mastering Insert Switchers

When working with audio, we need to work as fast and accurately as possible. Our hearing can become fatigued when listening with the required intensity, so I recommend using every tool to enable you to work as quickly as possible. I use an insert switcher to aid me as I work with hardware.

In a mastering setup, the inputs and outputs from your hardware are connected to the switcher alongside the inputs and outputs of the audio interface. In this configuration, the audio signal leaves the audio inter-face outputs and enters the switcher, travelling through the device before returning to the audio interface inputs. Hardware devices are connected to inputs and outputs throughout the circuit so you can insert your hardware into the signal path by pressing buttons on the switcher. Many switchers have between 4 and 8 push buttons on their fascia, permitting you to insert up to 8 pieces of hardware.

Most mastering switchers have more features, such as the ability to swap the order of the hardware, change the gain between left and right channels, access a mid-side matrix or send the signal to hardware rather than insert it.

I was naive initially and thought of them as simple controllers and luxury gadgets. But having used one for a few years, I couldn't work without one. The ability to quickly insert and remove a processor with a button is fundamental to my work. I currently use a Manley Backbone Mastering Insert Switcher, but we have a few switchers in the studio for mixing and mastering (Figure 4.2).

Figure 4.2 The Manley Backbone Insert Switcher.

Whether using software or hardware, I do recommend an insert switcher. This could be a hardware switcher such as the Manley Backbone or a software controller permitting you to insert and remove processing in your chain for immediate referencing. While you may believe you can accomplish this with a mouse, there is a substantial difference between simply pressing a button and having to move a mouse around. Our auditory memory can become fatigued fast, so we need to be able to compare audio efficiently.

Of course, there are further downsides to working with hardware. You need cables to connect everything, and this can be very expensive. I had custom EDAC (ELCO in the United States) cables made, which cost close to £800 for a couple of cables. However, they are an essential consideration when purchasing hardware.

Do not be caught out by the sales talk on cables, though. You do not need cables with special coatings, nor do they need to be gold-plated XLR cables. Much of the quality of cables is not from the cable itself but the terminating connectors.

The only exception to this rule are digital cables, particularly Thunderbolt cables. While paying £50 or more may seem expensive when they are available on Amazon for 10 times less, you would be surprised at the topology required for Thunderbolt. The more costly cables feature multiple microchips built into the connections to handle the bus speeds and decide which line to send the digital signal down. Cheaper cables are just wires and will not perform as well.

If you connect something as simple as a hard drive, cheaper cables are usually fine. Still, it is wise to invest if you are connecting technology that requires fast and efficient data transfer, such as Thunderbolt audio interfaces.

Recommended Processing

Whether you choose to use hardware, software or a mix of both, for basic mastering I recommend the following processors;

- EQ – Both dynamic and paragraphic (i.e., parametric)
- Mastering compressor
- Multi-band compressor
- Exciter
- De-Esser
- Stereo imager
- Limiter – Preferably with True Peak
- Metering – You will need VU and LUFS meters. These will be discussed later.

The software market is particularly volatile compared to hardware, and new products are released daily, so it would be erroneous to advise on any particular plug-ins to use. You must, however, ensure that they are all quality plug-ins because some will introduce quantisation, cramping and aliasing that will reduce the quality of the music you master.

You may have noticed that I recommended a de-esser in the mastering list; this is not by accident. Often, de-essing can provide better results for removing excessive high frequencies than relying on an EQ, which may introduce phase into the signal. While you could use a linear phase to reduce this, it also introduces ringing artefacts at a mix's extreme highs and lows.

Moreover, while there is software that offers an all-in-one solution, I don't personally recommend it. If we look at any hobby industry, regardless of what it is, when a manufacturer releases a product that caters for everything in one, it is usually poor as corners are cut somewhere. Furthermore, we've all heard the presets and sonic character from Izotope Ozone countless times, and many of us prefer to hear audio created from a mix and match of programs from different developers. There is a good reason that professionals do not rely on all-in-one programs.

Whether you run an entirely digital studio, a wholly analogue studio, or a hybrid studio, a final tool I recommend everyone invest in is a lava lamp.

These must be compulsory for any studio; I have yet to visit or work in any studio that does not have one. Even Trevor Horn has a lava lamp in his home studio.

The myth surrounding these is that they are considered lucky, but their real purpose is to act as a timer. They typically take 45 to 60 minutes to warm up (although this can be longer, depending on the room's temperature). Audio engineers realised that when a lava lamp was warm and the wax was free-forming, the tubes in the hardware had also reached the optimum temperature

Of course, if you're entirely in the digital domain, there are no valves to heat up, but they bring something else to a studio: a sense of peace and calm. I always refer to the metaphor of a doormat at the studio entrance. On this doormat, you wipe away all the outside world. It means that you don't bring in any distractions. One of the biggest distractions is time, and we have banned any form of physical clock in the studio. Having a lava lamp helps you further lose track of time.

Above all, however, you must understand and know your tools. You cannot expect to produce a good master if you don't know how your tools work on the audio. I don't mean just the quick start-up page or watching some presenter on YouTube; I mean reading the entire manual, experimenting, and listening to its effects on the audio, both positive and negative.

Depending on the software, this can take hours, days or weeks, but you must experiment and learn how it works. Push its limits and see how it fits into your workflow. This is the skill of a professional; they know exactly how the software (or hardware) operates the moment they instantiate it (or turn it on). You cannot master music successfully if every time you begin using a processor, you have to guess your way through it.

Chapter 5
Developing Listening Skills

Music and songs are believed to have been fundamental to our evolution. Indeed, several academics have suggested that humans sang as a form of communication before we even developed the capability of speech as we know it today. Over the centuries, our ear canal shape and hearing evolved, enhancing specific frequencies between the 1 to 5 kHz range.

We can refer to this range as the "Phonlea." It is an essential part of our species' fight-or-flight evolution, allowing us to perceive this specific frequency band to be louder than any others. This is particularly handy because it focuses on the human voice, making it easy to decipher critical areas of speech, amongst other noises.

Another enhanced frequency that the ear is sensitive to is 13.5 kHz; this is linked to the natural third harmonic resonance of the ear canal. An awareness of our uneven perception of frequencies highlights that we must concentrate harder than we initially think when listening for frequencies outside this phonlea range.

> Phonlea = Frequencies 1 to 5 kHz. The human hearing is sensitive to these frequencies.

As mastering engineers, we must listen critically and analytically to audio. You cannot access the individual stems at the mastering stage, only the stereo file. Therefore, you cannot solo individual tracks to check their quality; you must attune yourself to hear them within the context of the mix. This is far more difficult than it may sound.

DOI: 10.4324/9781032685229-6

I have been training my listening abilities for many years. As an audiologist, I would listen to audiometers, perform daily calibration checks using pure tones, listen to hearing aids and how they replicated environmental sounds and speech, and identify faults or minor distortions.

As I changed professions to work in music, I adapted my listening ability to identify different processing applied to audio, from reverberation to compression. Even now, I am constantly developing my listening skills, trying to hear further details in music or how a piece of hardware affects a sound. In many respects, ear training can be compared to actors regularly training at a gym. They must maintain their physique as part of their profession, and I must maintain my listening skills.

Over the years, I have used several ear training platforms, but none improved my hearing as they were too simple and aimed more towards rewarding listeners for accomplishing simple tasks. Instead, to train our ears for mastering, we must develop the ability to listen critically *and* analytically. Critical listening focuses on the technical aspects of the audio, such as the dynamic range, the tone of the instruments, possible distortions, panning, magnitude, and how the instruments blend. This can only be accomplished by intently listening to music and attempting to identify instruments, how they're played and where they sit in a mix.

Analytical listening is different and is more concerned with the emotional impact of the music and how it may evoke a feeling or meaning in the listener; this is more of a subjective form of listening. In many situations, you will be mastering music that does not exhibit the ambience for the genre, and in these instances, you must reinstate it.

All music exhibits ambience, sometimes called spectral balance; it describes music's overall spectral density and frequency distribution. Drum and bass, for example, has a very different ambience than House music, as the former contains more bass, more highs, and less midrange energy. Part of a mastering engineer's responsibility is to ensure that the music fits the ambience of the genre, which means that you must also understand the ambience of the genre you are working with.

While this may seem beyond the remit of any mastering engineer, they win awards for their technical ability *and* artistic input in mastering a track. To accomplish this, you must be willing to expose yourself to good quality music, know your tools, and develop your skills technically and artistically.

To help with this, I recommend developing a playlist of tracks produced/engineered to a high quality. This playlist might include tracks different from your taste or style, but exposing yourself to various well-produced tracks will help you develop your taste and appreciation of well-engineered and produced music. Listen to the emotional context of the track and how the instrument's tone and melody, alongside the overall ambience, help reinforce the music's message. I would not recommend listening to songs on Beatport for this, as there is a significant amount of amateur music on the platform. Instead, direct your focus towards pop music.

I listen to tracks from the early 1960s to the present day from various genres that have won awards or are critically acclaimed in the industry for their production values. You will develop a mature palette if you perform this as part of your continued professional development.

These techniques will help you develop analytical and critical skills. It is essential not to *shortcut* these abilities by following advice from YouTube presenters who advise using visual tools to see rather than hear problems in audio.

Our visual acuity will surpass our hearing ability every time. This is because visual cues help us understand language. When conversing with another person, we constantly look for visual clues to help us know what they say. The English language is mainly visual, and the shape of the mouth or hand gestures will help us further determine what is being said. This is why you should not cover your mouth when you are talking. Otherwise, it makes it difficult for the listener to hear you.

You can find evidence of visuals eclipsing our hearing everywhere. It is an auditory illusion known as the McGurk Effect, which you can try. Speak to someone and say, "How bar is the journey?" while covering your mouth, and they will hear how far the journey is. Repeat the same, but this time, uncover your mouth, and they will hear how bar is the journey.

There are many examples of the McGurk effect on the internet, and you will have experienced it at one time or another. I have often found myself adjusting parameters on hardware, believing I can hear the difference before realising the hardware is bypassed.

You should be aware of this effect if you use any visual software designed to show problems in the audio. While we have to rely on software to help us determine and validate some issues, such as a mix that leans slightly to the left or right, we should not rely solely on it. This is particularly the case with using an FFT to inform us of any problematic frequencies in a mix for reasons discussed later.

A final benefit of ear training is that it will help us develop our auditory memory. Audio is heard independently by each ear and is stored in the brain for approximately 4 to 10 seconds. This is known as Echoic memory and helps us process pitch and localisation in situations where the audio is instantaneous and transient.

We must develop our short – and long-term auditory memory (STM and LTM) for audio engineering because it will improve our critical and analytical listening skills. This skill is essential for any producer or engineer, allowing us to recall what we have heard without referencing it.

Indeed, one of the worst pieces of advice is to import a track into your DAW to reference for mastering. No two tracks are ever the same (nor should they be), and placing a reference in your DAW to continually draw from will lead to a poor master because you will naturally attempt to match the music in terms of spectral balance and dynamics.

For example, two house tracks will be entirely different spectrally despite being in the same genre. The composition, arrangement, and sound design will always differ from one track to another. Suppose one house track features a low-frequency kick with a long amplitude decay but a short high-frequency bass, and the track you are mastering features a low-frequency bass with a short decay but a light kick with a longer decay. In that case, they are two entirely different balances in frequency and dynamics. While both are house music, the results would be terrible if you attempted to use it as a reference and imply that ambience to yours.

Furthermore, the reference track is likely an MP3; this compressed format uses filters to remove frequencies it believes you cannot hear, which introduces phase distortion, so you're likely also using a distorted piece of music to reference against. I cannot think of one professional who instantiates a reference track because they don't know how a master should sound.

I'm not suggesting you should never use reference tracks; listening to several tracks in the genre can be beneficial *before* you begin to master, but you should use your aural memory to master and not rely on a direct reference. If you are not yet skilled enough to do this, you must accept you do not yet have the necessary skills to master music.

Ear Fatigue and Protection

I would be remiss to conclude this chapter on listening without discussing the importance of looking after our ears. They are our primary tools, and we must care for and protect them. If our hearing is damaged, no magic pill will ever restore it, and hearing aids will not provide the detail you need to work with music.

Listening to audio at a high amplitude will produce an "eargasm", an excitement that can result in piloerection (hairs on your arm standing on edge). This is the stimulation of the Cochlea's basilar membrane, lined with a series of hair cells that, when triggered into motion, deliver neurons to the brain's auditory part, releasing endorphins, the feel-good chemicals in our brains.

The basilar membrane area is susceptible to lower frequencies, and as the wavelength is long, we can feel it, too, which explains why we love a low-rumbling bass. Moreover, listening to loud bass music will also increase the heart rate, which is why it is so prevalent in gyms.

While we may feel we need to listen to dance music at a loud volume to master it, this isn't the case. It only results in ear fatigue occurring twice as fast, and as soon as this happens, we will begin to add further processing to make the music exciting again. This results in over-processing and a master that commonly sounds like a brick wall of sound.

Instead, we should monitor the music at a quieter volume, approximately 60 to 70 dB SPL and only occasionally increase the volume for a short period to check how it sounds. While I suspect many readers of this do not have access to a sound meter, apps available for both iOS and Android can act as an SPL meter. If you don't have access to a smartphone, you can compare the audio to conversational speech, which is also approximately 60 dB.

It is advisable to also take regular breaks from listening. As you become more experienced, you will find that you can listen for longer, but as a rule of thumb, a break every 20 to 30 minutes is preferable and will help prevent ear fatigue.

I also recommend investing in some hearing protection. I'm often surprised by the number of professionals who do not have any custom hearing protection but regularly expose themselves to loud noises (clubs, festivals, etc.) that can result in permanent hearing damage. It isn't cheap, but considering the cost divided by the number of years, it will last and protect your most vital tool; they are worth what you pay.

Chapter 6

Bit Depth, Sample Rates, Aliasing, and Dither

I would assume most readers of this book are producers already aware of both bit depth and sample rates. However, it would be remiss of me to leave it out from a book on mastering as they play an essential role in both production *and* mastering. Indeed, understanding both sample rates and bit depth is essential for any mastering engineer as we need to ensure we do not accidentally introduce aliasing or inter-sample peaks on the material we're working with.

In the digital realm, audio is represented by two measurements: time and amplitude. Amplitude is recorded digitally as a series of discrete measurements, or steps, stored in the digital device as binary digits, known as bits. These bits are based on exponential math; therefore, 16 bits equal 65,536 discrete measurements, and 24-bit offers over 16 million measurements (Figure 6.1).

The greater the bit depth, the more information is available to represent the amplitude of the audio. This could be compared to a digital image; the more pixels in the picture, the more precise and more defined it is; similarly, the more measurements we take for the bit depth, the more precise the waveform representation within the digital domain.

This is important because analogue waveforms are free-flowing and change continuously. If an amplitude change occurs between one of the bit measurements, the digital recording device must either round up or round down to the subsequent nearest measurement. Thus, the fewer bits available, the more the interface has to round up or down, and the more noticeable it becomes.

DOI: 10.4324/9781032685229-7

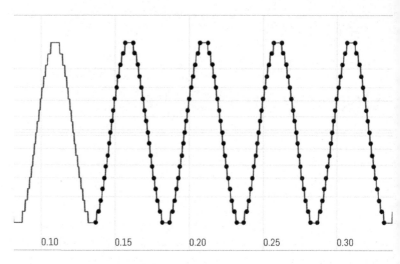

Figure 6.1 The Bit depth in this example is low, showing how it may affect the waveform.

Inaccurate waveform representation caused by too few bits is known as quantisation error. This is a problematic distortion to describe, but as all DAWs now come with bit-crusher plug-ins, I recommend placing it on an audio channel and reducing the bits so you can hear the effects. Notably, while bit depths of 12-bit or higher may seem inaudible, the impact is worsened as further channels are mixed together.

Each bit represents 6 dBs of dynamic range, and many processes, such as mixing (summing individual channels together), editing audio, or applying plug-ins, affect the dynamic range of the audio. This can begin to introduce quantisation errors. Indeed, many early DAWs had a fixed-point bit depth, and you could hear the quantisation noise on the reverb tails as it began to fall towards silence (known as the RT60). This could also cause problems during the mastering process because as we applied dynamic restriction via plug-ins, it often introduced quantisation noise (Figure 6.2).

Most audio interfaces available now are 24-bit, and recently, 32-bit interfaces have started to appear, so it's unlikely that you'll experience quantisation error from recording, provided you record at the highest depth available. DAWs also use floating point algorithms of 32 or 64 bits. This increases the bit depth of the audio, significantly reducing

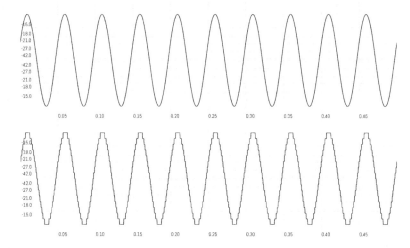

Figure 6.2 Quantisation errors. Note how the lower waveform is not accurately represented.

the introduction of quantisation error from applying plug-ins due to a much higher dynamic range.

This is not to suggest it cannot happen, though. Not all plug-ins are equal, and many lower-quality examples exhibit poor implementation of low-frequency filters that introduce noise. Thus, you must be cautious of what tools you use for mastering!

Quantisation errors can also occur when the audio's bit rate is reduced to be compatible with some playback devices. While many devices operate at 24-bit, if you want to print the music to CD, this has a 16-bit limitation, and therefore, you must reduce the bit rate further.

Reducing the bit depth requires a process called dithering. As we reduce the bit depth, we use fewer measurements to represent the amplitude. Therefore, there is more rounding up (or down) of the audio signal, which can introduce quantisation noise. While we cannot avoid this, we can disguise it by randomising these errors using low-level white noise. By applying the noise, the reduction of bits becomes more random, camouflaging any errors.

Of course, this may beg the question, can we hear dither?

While some engineers suggest they can hear it, I argue that very few individuals can. The noise added by dither is approximately 3 dB above the noise floor on a 16-bit file, effectively 93 dB below the peak level. It may be perceptible in extreme circumstances, such as a song that ends with a reverb tail, but as humans, we're good at ignoring random noise.

Indeed, it may be worth using a different dithering algorithm if you can hear it. Dithering algorithms use various types of noise shaping, effectively using an EQ to modify the noise in the algorithm. In my experience, it's difficult to tell the difference between the different types of dithers, but in some instances, one may sound better. You will need to experiment with the various types available.

A question often posed during mastering is whether we need to dither from the DAW's 32-bit or 64-bit floating point to a 24-bit file for delivery to labels and streaming services. The answer really depends on the audio and the DAW you're using. Most DAWs will not permit you to print audio above 0 dBFS; therefore, working at 32-bit, you would not need to dither. However, it would be essential to dither if the DAW permits you to print the audio above 0 dBFS or if you're working at 64 bits.

The reasons for this relates to mathematical calculations performed in the DAW, which are below if you're interested. For many, though, if you're not studying for a master's degree, feel free to skip the following two paragraphs.

32-bit floating point is a single precision consisting of three components: a 23-bit mantissa, an 8-bit exponent, and a 1-bit sign. Here, the bit resolution in 32 bits is only 23 bits compared to the 24 bits of the audio file, which is a fixed point. These additional bits are only present in the DAW to scale precision when calculating large numbers to minimise rounding errors.

Since digital audio is typically scaled within -1, 0 to 1, 0 (0 dBFS), the information is multiplied by one, making it identical, so dithering would not necessarily be required. However, if the DAW permits you to export above 0 dBFS (1,0 floating point), you would need to dither because the DAW has to reassign higher than the peak. That said, exporting a delivery format higher than 0 dBFS wouldn't make much sense because it will distort D/A conversion (True Peak value).

If you choose to work in a 64-bit floating point in your DAW, though, the mantissa is now 52-bit long with an 11-bit exponent and 1-bit sign, so you probably need to use dithering when bouncing to a 24-bit fixed point, depending on the DAW.

Sample Rate

Alongside amplitude, we also require a measurement over time, known as the sample rate. This is the number of times a measurement of the analogue waveform is taken per second. The number of samples taken must be enough to accurately replicate the waveform in the digital realm, as defined by the Whittaker–Nyquist–Shannon theorem.

The theorem states that to accurately replicate an analogue waveform in the digital domain, a measurement must be taken twice the analogue signal's frequency. If the sample rate is any less, it will be reproduced at a lower frequency, becoming an "alias" of the original audio. That's the theory; more measurements are required in practice due to the finite time available (Figure 6.3).

This misrepresentation of a signal from an inadequate sampling frequency will create additional harmonics below the original frequency, resulting in unwanted artefacts. While these are typically low in amplitude, they will reduce the clarity of a mix. This is an important consideration when applying any form of saturation via a plug-in.

Some engineers like to apply saturation effects when mastering to add warmth, smoothness, body, and several other descriptive words. The problem with this approach is that the additional harmonics generated by the plug-in will easily exceed the Nyquist on many masters, which can result in aliasing.

For example, many saturation plug-ins add second-order harmonic distortion to a signal because this replicates the sounds of tubes, adding thickness and warmth. To accomplish this, it will multiply the incoming signal by x2, x4, x6, x8, x10, x12, and so forth. If we multiply a single harmonic occurring at 15 kHz by x2, then x4, etc., the additional harmonics generated will likely exceed the Nyquist of the digital system.

15 kHz x 2 = 30 kHz
15 kHz x 4 = 60 kHz
15 kHz x 6 = 90 kHz
15 kHz x 8 = 120 kHz
15 kHz x 10 = 150 kHz
15 kHz x 12 = 180 kHz
15 kHz x 14 = 210 kHz

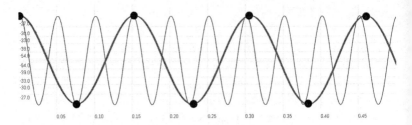

Figure 6.3 The effects of aliasing. When two points are not measured accurately, a lower-frequency alias of the waveform will be generated.

As shown, all of these additional harmonics generated by saturation can quickly exceed the Nyquist, resulting in aliases appearing in the audible range of the music. Moreover, this is one singular frequency. If we consider that you are working on a stereo mix consisting of multiple frequencies across the spectra up to 20 kHz, it can cause significant problems.

This is not to suggest we should never employ saturation. Aliasing is not always a problem; it depends entirely on the frequency at which it occurs. Sometimes, it can add thickness, presence, and body, but in others, it can result in significant problems that impact the spectral density and balance of the music. If I apply saturation to a master, I do so through hardware, as the analogue to digital anti-aliasing filters on my converters ensure that nothing occurs beyond the Nyquist, removing the opportunity for aliasing in the digital domain.

Another consideration is frequency cramping, which occurs at higher frequencies when using a bell curve EQ. As we hit the Nyquist Theorem, the EQ bell curve will become uneven, resulting in an effect we call cramping. This produces a brittle sound in the higher frequencies.

This can be highly unpleasant, particularly when experienced through headphones. Although some claim that the average "Joe Public" listener will not hear it or even care if it's present, it doesn't mean we shouldn't take pride in our work. Many of the more prominent labels who sign music have experience in music production, and they will notice amateur mistakes like this and will not look favourably upon it.

We have a few options to prevent this frequency cramping. The first is to use hardware EQ because there is no Nyquist in the analogue

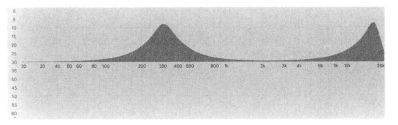

Figure 6.4 The effects of frequency cramping. Note how the bell curve is distorted once we reach the Nyquist.

domain, and the conversion from analogue to digital employs anti-aliasing filters. If you are restricted by budget or real estate in your studio, choose a suitable digital EQ or use a shelving filter.

Shelving is the easiest way to deal with EQ adjustments in the higher frequencies, and some EQs, such as the Harrison 32C EQ, default to a shelf when you draw close to the Nyquist. Other EQs are designed to prevent frequency cramping, so you should investigate and read the manual of any EQ you use for mastering to ensure it can deal appropriately with the material.

Alternatively, you can always increase your project's sampling rate. However, due to the filters involved, upscaling and downscaling an audio file may add unwanted artefacts to the audio. Ideally, you should always use the supplied file and not adjust the sample or bit depth (Figure 6.4).

Chapter 7
Dynamics

When mastering EDM, many prioritise making the music as loud as possible. This is because mastering is the final stage, during which you would typically receive a mastering engineer's objective opinion on the music's spectral balance and weight. However, when mastering yourself, you do not have this objective view; therefore, all that is left is loudness. This is why many articles, forum users, and presenters are concerned with loudness rather than anything else.

Of course, when we experience music, we will always perceive any that is louder to sound better, but what about when it is listened to quietly? Good music is good *regardless* of its playback volume, and it'll simply sound even better when, or if, it is *played* louder.

Note that I said *played* louder, not *created* louder. Heavily restricted music for increased volume perception can make good music sound bad. And lousy music, well, that will remain bad regardless of its playback volume. Indeed, at the risk of upsetting the plastic producers who write articles or create video content rather than produce music, most professional DJs have access to volume parameters, and good ones know how to use them. There is no point in creating a great piece of music to then ruin it by crushing it to death. Indeed, dynamics are essential for music, but before we examine them in any detail, we should discuss how they are measured in mastering.

Our perception of volume changes with frequency. The exact frequency range that humans are sensitive to will vary depending on the research you refer to, though it is essentially the range of the human voice calling for help or an infant's cry. I refer to this range as the "Phonlea."

DOI: 10.4324/9781032685229-8

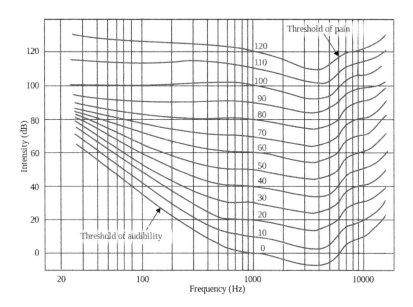

Figure 7.1 Fletcher Munson curve.

This forms an essential part of our species' fight-or-flight evolution. Hearing the human voice over our environment or possible dangers is critical to survival. I'd rather my partner hear my screams about a spider in the bedroom over the coffee machine any day. The Fletcher Munson Curve, published in 1933, was the first to illustrate this phenomenon (our perception changing with frequency, not spiders in the bedroom) (Figure 7.1).

Notably, this curve was later considered inaccurate because the tests were conducted with headphones, which changes how we perceive frequencies depending on how they're worn. Thus, it has since been superseded by the New International Standards (ISO 226:2003), but regardless, their initial discoveries led to our understanding of how our perception changes with frequency.

When measuring sound, this perception change means we must use meters with filters to mimic the human ear's response to stimuli for a more meaningful measurement. For example, an A-weighting filter mimics the ear's response to sounds at normal listening levels, while C-weighting mimics the ear's response at increased volumes. Others, such as Z-weighting, have no filter applied. These filters are used in different circumstances depending on what is being measured and its purpose. For instance, when calculating the noise floor of audio equipment, we typically use an A-weighted.

When measuring *perceived* volume, things become a little more tricky. While amplitude can be measured in decibels, loudness is unquantifiable and relative to the listener. What is loud to me may be quiet to you.

Bob Katz, a mastering engineer, was the first to approach a new measurement format using what is known as a K-system before the international audio standard organisations invented LUFS to measure loudness. This format uses what we call a K-weighted filter.

K-weighting is similar to A-weighting. It uses a filter to mimic the human perception of sound by rolling off the low frequencies below 100 Hz. However, K-weighting provides a slight gain boost above 2 kHz. This filter enables us to reasonably determine how loud the "average" person would p*erceive* a piece of music. This K-weighting forms the foundation of LUFS measurements.

Loudness **U**nits **F**ull **S**cale is a relatively new measurement system developed in 2011 to help deal with TV advertisements being louder than TV programs. Advertisements were always louder because advertising companies pushed limiters to the maximum so that the loudness would grab our attention—even if we were in the next room making a coffee during the ad break.

LUFS measurements are now used for audio normalisation in television broadcasts, so all advertisements and programming must conform to this new measurement making adverts roughly the same volume as the program. Or at least that was the aim; if you've ever experienced the "forced" adverts on Amazon Prime, someone forgot to inform them of the standard.

Streaming services such as Spotify, Apple, Tidal, and Pandora have also adopted this standard and employ "loudness penalties" if the music is too loud. If your music exhibits a high RMS value from excessive limiting, it will reduce the amplitude to approximately the same volume as all other music on the service.

This provides a comfortable listening environment for all users, saving us from having to adjust the volume for each track we listen to. It could be seen as a virtual mastering engineer balancing and ensuring all levels are the same on an album. Therefore, LUFS are an excellent system to understand and work with, and many mastering engineers have adopted it as a reference measurement.

I say many, but not all, because the LUFS system is not a "required" standard for mastering. Indeed, there is no requirement to follow any standards in mastering for streaming services; you're free to do whatever you feel is right. However, many professional mastering engineers have adopted the LUFS measurement because it helps us ensure the music is "compatible" with streaming services. A heavily limited mix with restricted dynamics will sound terrible played at a lower volume compared to a mix with plenty of dynamics.

When working in LUFS, there are two values: short-term (S)LUFS and integrated (I)LUFS. Short-term LUFS is a measurement taken over three seconds of audio, whereas (I)LUFS are calculated over the entirety of the audio file. As with most measurements in audio, LUFS is measured in a negative value, with zero as the reference point for the measurement, and therefore, the lower the LUFS value, the louder the *average* person will perceive the music. Thus, -16 LUFS is perceivably quieter than -9 LUFS.

When mastering, it's tempting to take the easy route and search online to find out what LUFS value we should use for music. The problem is, while broadcast has standards, music does not. Therefore, many articles, blogs, forums, and presenters will offer a various range of values they *think* you should aim for, which ranges from -14 (fairly quiet) to -5 (I)LUFS (very loud).

Alternatively, some chose to measure their favourite songs' (I)LUFS and use that result as a reference. While this may appear to be the sensible option and provide golden figures to aim for, they are only a tiny part of a much larger puzzle.

For many listeners, part of the magic of listening to electronic dance music (EDM) is what they experience in a club or festival environment: the kick punching them in the chest and the bass frequencies flapping their trousers and kick drums pounding their chest.

As mentioned in the earlier chapter, the punch of EDM results from how much louder the kick is (the peak value) from the body of the music (the RMS value). The difference between the RMS and Peak Values of the music is known as the crest factor in mastering.

This is important because the higher this figure is, the more dynamics there are in the music, and the louder the kick will appear due to the increased peak-to-RMS ratio. We can measure the dynamic value between RMS and peak amplitude to obtain the crest factor via the following;

$$\text{Peak} = -1$$
$$\text{RMS} = -13$$
$$\text{C} / \text{F} = -1 - (-13) = 12$$

If there is a significant crest factor, the kick will punch hard because it moves the cone further in relation to its RMS value. However, the bass will not be as present if there is a high crest factor.

This is because a trouser-flapping bass requires sustained activity, which contributes to the music's RMS value. Producers often face this dilemma while creating music and commonly reach for the cheapest, easiest option: side-chaining or volume ducking.

Numerous plug-ins are now available designed to perform little more than modulate the amplitude of a signal. Producers insert these onto the bass channel so that every time the kick occurs, the bass temporarily drops in amplitude, allowing the kick to pull through and not interfere with the bass.

As this is a book on mastering, I'm not going to comment on the absurdity of maintaining a bass presence in two instruments, but suffice to say that amplitude modulation is a form of synthesis that generates additional harmonics on either side of the original harmonics. Figure 7.2 shows a sine wave measured in an FFT, followed by the additional sidebands generated by amplitude modulating only this sine wave.

If we consider that a bass consists of many more harmonics, each will be subjected to side-band information. The energy created by these occurring below the fundamental of the bass creates significant low-frequency issues. Many mastering engineers often have to deal with this problem due to poor advice from media outlets.

Indeed, I have witnessed some engineers use this form of amplitude modulation during mastering to allow for punch *and* energy, utterly unaware that the sidebands generated across the frequency range significantly harm the material. Only when played via a club or festival do they realise how bad the music now sounds.

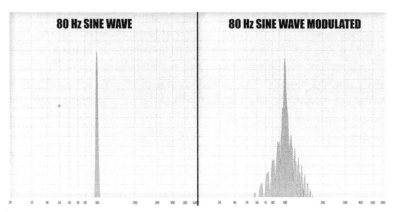

Figure 7.2 The effects of amplitude modulation side-chaining.

During mastering, we need to retain the dynamics but also want the bass to be present. While a heavily limited mix will sound OK loud in a club (albeit lacking punch), it will not translate well when it's reduced in volume to match other records on streaming services. Indeed, music lacking in dynamics often transforms into a dull, flat, lifeless piece of music when streamed, making it more likely to result in a listener skipping your track.

While you may not be interested in your track translating well on streaming services because you're writing music for clubs, you're choosing to ignore over 600 million potential listeners. In many countries, DJs do not pay you royalties; streaming services do.

Professional EDM mastering, therefore, becomes a balancing act. Of course, this is nothing new because transfer engineers have been doing it since the 1940s; we can never know how any one person may choose to experience music. But this is the art of mastering, performing a careful balancing act so that the track sounds acceptable on streaming services, headphones, or earbuds at lower volumes but sits well with every other record when played at clubs on large monitor speakers.

Dynamic Solutions

The easiest way to deal with the problem would be to master two versions. I have sometimes had the opportunity to address these issues when supplied with two versions of the same track.

A few artists recognise that streaming service tracks should be shorter because nobody wants to listen to a two-minute drum loop intro in their home. Unlike during the vinyl years when you would have to get off your ass to move the needle to skip a track, today, it's a button press away, and the streaming generation has a short attention span. Yet, in a club, it's an entirely different story. A DJ expects a two or three-minute intro to mix in the record.

Therefore, occasionally, I receive two versions of a track to master, and I approach each slightly differently. The shorter track is mastered for the streaming platforms. By employing a higher crest factor in the music, if the streaming service turns the music down to match other records, it maintains a dynamic edge, making the music sound vibrant and punchy.

The DJ or more extended club version is slightly more restricted/limited during mastering. This reduces the crest factor slightly but maintains punch while making the music perceivably louder. This way, the DJ does not have to use the volume control on their decks. After all, some prefer to perform, dance, wave their arms around, fake turn their parameters, act as though they are electrified, or throw cakes at the clubbers. As EDM mastering engineers, we could make our lives easier if there was an industry-recognised DJ mastering level (DJML) or DJ wave level (DJWL).

However, if you only have one mix, we must approach any dynamic manipulation cautiously. Maintaining punch and volume requires a blend of compression, saturation, clipping, and limiting. While applying these, keeping an eye on your levels to remain within streaming service guidelines is vital. Streaming services operate at specific (I)LUFS values, and I recommended using a plugin to enable you to monitor your audio values so you can compare.

- Spotify: -14 LUFS (Integrated)
- Apple Music: -16 LUFS (Integrated)
- YouTube: -14 LUFS (Integrated)
- Tidal: -14 LUFS (Integrated)
- Amazon Music: -14 LUFS (Integrated)
- Deezer: -15 LUFS (Integrated)

Several commercially available plugins exist, including "ADPTR Audio's Streamliner" (Figure 7.3). I will not explain how this plugin works; ADPTR

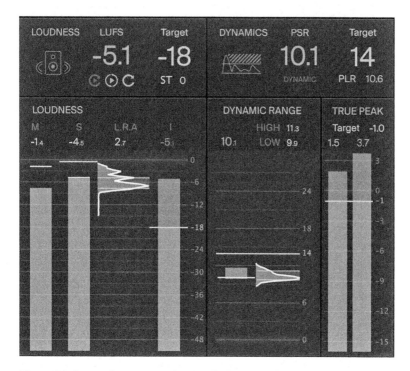

Figure 7.3 Streamliner measuring the PLR and PSR values.

Audio has a manual available online for download. If you decide to use it, I recommend (and hope) you read it, but I want to highlight some specific values on its interface (Figure 7.3).

The most important values are the PSR and PLR, not the LUFS. The design team at "Meter Plugs" conceived PLR and PSR for the dynameter plugin. They wanted a term to describe a measurement similar to a crest factor value but based on an international loudness standard (ITU BS.1770). They coined the peak short-term loudness ratio (PSR) and peak long-term loudness ratio (PLR).

The PLR measures the whole track, while the PSR is a real-time three-second audio window. Note that the PSR and PLR are not dB values, as they are measurements taken over time but I aim for a PLR value no lower than seven for most EDM genres during mastering. A value of 7 (or higher) PLR tends to provide a good balance between the kick that maintains its punch and a bass that will flap your trousers.

The PSR will vary dramatically throughout the track from loud to competitive to dynamic, and you must monitor this measurement continually. However, it can be helpful when referring to a section of your track that might be heavily compressed. Ensuring that the value for this section does not linger in the loud range (5 to 7 PSR) will mean that some dynamics have been maintained.

As mentioned, both of these values are more important than the LUFS. Indeed, when I'm mastering, I do not aim for a specific LUFS value; instead, I aim for the loudest possible master while also maintaining the dynamics. The resulting integrated LUFS becomes immaterial because there is no point in striving for some fictional gold standard LUFS value if your music sounds completely crushed and translates poorly on playback.

Indeed, we must always consider how the speaker monitors will translate the audio waveform because these are ultimately the only components that matter in our chain. If the speaker monitors can translate the music coherently, it will sound better to the public. I always recommend looking at the waveform and translating its changing structure to the motion of the speaker cone. The speaker driver will behave the same if the waveform resembles a sausage.

I've found that when I'm working to keep the PSR at 7, most EDM music tends to balance out at around -10 (I)LUFS. This usually maintains an excellent overall volume with an adequate crest factor. However, as important as all this metering is, it is far more critical that we use our ears and listen to the results. All music is different, and sometimes, you may find that while attaining good values throughout, the music still sounds overly limited or squashed.

This can result from heavy-handed compression, saturation, clipping, signal density from the production process or the arrangement of the music itself. Our perception of volume changes not only with frequency but also with time. We will perceive timbres that sustain to be louder than those that do not. Therefore, a peak timbre, like a kick drum, will sound quieter than a sustained bass note despite sharing the same amplitude. We must consider if compression has been excessively used during production, as that can change peak values to RMS, which will always influence the metering results.

Chapter 8
Mastering EQ

EQ during the mastering stage differs from EQ performed at the production stage. As a mastering engineer, you are no longer dealing with
individual tracks of instruments or effects but with a single stereo audio
file. Therefore, even minor adjustments at a limited band of frequencies
will affect the rest of the file. To understand why this happens, we need
to investigate EQ.

I'm positive that many readers already understand the concept of
phase. If we have two identical signals and we shift the timing of one,
phasing will be introduced between the two. This is because as the
cycle of one wave rises, the secondary signal may fall, and if these two
signals are 180 degrees out of phase with one another, they will cancel
each other out.

EQ works on a similar principle. Audio signals in the analogue realm
are AC signals. Running these through capacitors and inductors to
delay the signal in time and feed back into the input results in an adjustment of phase against the original signal. Combining an unaltered signal with a phase-shifted version of itself cancels some of the signal.

Digital EQ uses a similar method, although it uses a digital delay line
rather than capacitors and inductors. Feeding these delays back into
the input and reversing their polarity will create cuts and boosts.

Whether analogue or digital, the critical thing to note is that EQ is
accomplished via shifting the signal phase, a process known as minimal phase EQ or an infinite impulse response (IIR) filter. This phase
adjustment is well suited for mixing duties when working with individual

DOI: 10.4324/9781032685229-9

instruments because it adds a perceivably attractive colouration to the audio signal. Still, it can sometimes cause problems when working on a complete mix. Excessive phase shifts in stereo material can do more harm than good because they affect the frequencies on either side of the EQ adjustments, and this becomes more noticeable the higher the Q value becomes.

Lower Q values affect more frequencies on either side of the central frequency. This means that the phase introduced by an analogue EQ (or IIR digital EQ) tends to be disguised, particularly if the cuts or boosts are less than a few decibels.

Higher Q values (i.e. more surgical alterations) become more noticeable because fewer frequencies are affected on either side, and the phasing becomes more evident, especially on complex signals such as a complete mix. In this instance, we should use a linear phase EQ. These work in the same manner as minimal phase EQ but with one crucial difference: the unaffected signal is delayed in time, so it meets with the phase delayed signal, ensuring that all frequencies arrive at the output simultaneously.

Delaying the entire signal results in some latency that must be corrected; therefore, this can only be accomplished via a digital EQ. These are called finite impulse response (FIR) or linear phase EQs. However, while these are more suitable to more surgical corrections, they are susceptible to audible ringing and pre-echo.

Pre-echo and ringing are just another term for oscillation. We can compare ringing in an EQ to holding a microphone next to a speaker and monitoring its output. You'll have witnessed it somewhere, even if you haven't experienced it personally. As soon as the microphone comes too close to the speaker, there is a howl round, a loud whistling tone. This oscillation (or ringing) is the result of feedback. Some producers may recognise this effect as the filter resonance on a synthesiser self-oscillating and producing a sine wave.

As EQ uses a similar feedback principle as resonance, a poor phase response from positive feedback can produce a ringing effect from the EQ. The ringing isn't loud, and you have to listen closely to hear it, but it can cause harm to the material. Notably, this ringing occurs with both minimal *and* linear phase EQ, although it is often indistinguishable with minimal phase EQs because the timing differences mask it. This is not the case with linear phase; therefore, it can be more noticeable.

With this in mind, we should choose the EQ depending on what we want to accomplish. Minimal phase EQ only adjusts the timing relationship between the *modified frequencies*, but the linear phase maintains the timing relationship between *all the frequencies*. Both, however, will alter the signal's phase and exhibit phase distortion.

Therefore, if the material requires wide-band adjustments (smaller Q values), a minimal phase is generally preferred. In contrast, a linear phase may be preferred if it requires surgical adjustments. In both cases, you must listen to whether the phase damages the material (minimal) or the ringing does (linear).

Every process in audio engineering has a trade-off, and we must carefully consider the consequences. Indeed, this is one of the main lessons of mastering; rather than looking for reasons to apply any processing, we should find reasons not to. If we must use it, we consider what we may be introducing into the material and if it is worth the cost.

Approaching EQ in Mastering

To employ EQ in mastering, I first listen to the material from beginning to end. My attention is on listening for any resonant frequencies in the mix. These can be identified as a sharp whistle-type tone occurring in the music. Typically, these occur at around 320, 800 Hz, 1, 1.2, 1.6, 2, 2.4, 3.1, 4, and 6.4 kHz.

I understand this may seem bizarrely specific, but repeatedly, over many mastering sessions, I've found myself having to correct resonances occurring in these areas. I'm not suggesting they do not happen elsewhere; I will listen for resonances occurring at *any* frequency, but those mentioned above often appear in all EDM genres. I believe these are a result of poor monitoring environments, room resonances, the use of synthesiser presets (many exhibit excessive energy between 1kHz to 6kHz because it is easy to hear), and the heavy-handed use of dynamic processing (which introduces sidebands) and further processors that introduce aliasing.

I will use a linear phase EQ to solve resonant problems, using a high Q value of 30 or above and placing a cut of approximately 2 to 5 dB. My tool is the FabFilter ProQ3, but you can use any EQ that does not negatively affect the audio too strongly.

Often, information online suggests using a high Q value and boosting frequencies to find resonances, but this is a terrible idea. Boosting any frequency with a high Q value will bring out resonance at *any* frequency, problematic or not. Sounds consist of multiple sine waves, all occurring at different frequencies and amplitudes across the spectra, and boosting any one of these will produce a sine wave that sounds like resonance. You must learn to listen and identify them without increasing the frequency range.

If possible, I will set the EQ to dynamic so it's inconsistent across the mix. Indeed, I often find that the resonance may only occur at specific points in the music, such as at the cadence or when the harmony of the music changes. While I'm optimistic that many reading this know dynamic EQ, for those unaware, it acts like a compressor, only activating when a threshold is breached (Figure 8.1).

To use a dynamic EQ, you can place a cut with a high Q value of about 4 dB into the material and then adjust the threshold. The threshold setting depends on the material, but the EQ will begin as the resonance breaches the threshold. You adjust the threshold enough to reduce the resonance but not so that the EQ consistently acts on the music.

In either case, remember that linear phase EQ can introduce ringing, so after every adjustment, it is essential to bypass the EQ and

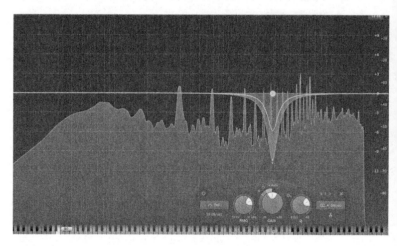

Figure 8.1 Using dynamic EQ in a master.

listen for the differences. Mastering is about avoiding processing rather than applying, so it is important not to get carried away.

Once all the resonances are dealt with, I often send the material out of the box into analogue EQ because I intend to use broader Q values. If you are working entirely in the box, you will typically want to use a minimal-phase EQ. The purpose here is to make minor cuts or boosts of only a few dB with a low Q value to ensure that the material conforms (in some respects) to the ambience of the genre.

I've discussed ambience in a previous chapter, but to refresh those who speed read or jumped straight to the practical application of mastering, ambience describes the music's overall spectral density and frequency distribution. Drum and bass, for example, exhibits a different ambience than House music, as the former contains more bass, more highs, and less mid-range energy.

Some mastering engineers may use a graphic EQ for these adjustments. These feature fixed bands that can be attenuated or increased. Typically, mastering graphic EQs have 26 or 32 bands, which enables the engineer to perform precise processing. The Q on these is fixed and remains constant, but they often rely on the Mel spectrum.

The Mel spectrum consists of EQ bands modelled on the ear, each making a perceptual difference. Adjusting bands between these does not significantly affect what we hear and is often considered unnecessary. Some software can also behave the same, such as Eventides Equivocate. This graphic EQ is based on the Mel scale, employing a linear phase filter shape to reduce ringing while also permitting you to match the ambience of one track to another (Figure 8.2).

I prefer a standard minimal phase EQ for these corrections rather than the graphic approach, but my process should not influence your decisions. Mastering is about developing your techniques and ensuring the music plays adequately on as many systems as possible. Another option to consider here, however, is whether to use passive or active EQ.

I usually employ a passive EQ, such as the SPL PASSEQ. The difference between a passive and active EQ is whether or not the circuits require amplification. A passive EQ boosts material by reducing the amplitude of frequencies on either side of the frequency you're adjusting, whereas an active EQ will amplify the selected frequencies.

While this difference may appear inconsequential, the topology significantly influences the material. An active EQ will generally add some

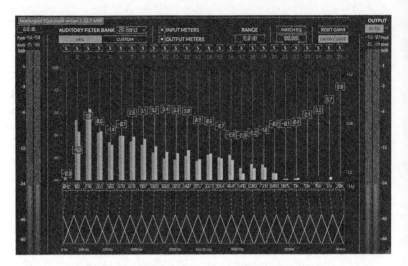

Figure 8.2 Eventide Equivocate. A graphic EQ based on the Mel scale.

colour to the signal (which may or may not be wanted), but it may also affect the material's transient response. I often find that active EQs reduce the transient information slightly, which can affect the positioning of instruments. Passive EQs will maintain this transient response, tend to sound cleaner, and, frequently, are more musical.

To my ears, a passive EQ often sounds far better than an active one on the lower and higher frequencies, while an active EQ often sounds better for the midrange. Despite most of the fundamental energy being contained in the midrange and active EQs slurring them slightly, it adds a sense of cohesion that doesn't work as well in the lower registers.

The first EQ I usually reach for is the Charteroak PEQ-1. If using software, I recommend that you select a minimal-phase EQ. For this process, you want an EQ with an extensive range of bands to choose from, and I like the combination of the Charteroak PEQ-1 followed by an API 5500.

The Charteroak PEQ-1 is a stereo-tone controller that I use to enhance the tonal balance of the music, particularly in the midrange. Although it's a natural phase EQ, it offers a broad Q designed with the natural resonances of the ear and our hearing range. I find using an API 5500 afterwards to attenuate or boost ensures that the processing of the Charteroak PEQ-1 adds is controlled.

I would typically follow this with a passive EQ, such as the SPL PASSEQ. I like using the passive EQ to work on the lower and higher frequencies. Active EQ's often distort or smear the lower frequencies, adding a boxy nature to the sound. A passive EQ adds a sense of warmth and musical cohesion.

The biggest problem with the lower frequencies is whether the artist has employed side-chaining or volume-pumping tools, which cause significant issues with a mix's low frequencies. If they have followed the "advice" of presenters that the bass should be side-chained to the kick, there will be excessive low-end energy. This is because side-chaining generates side-band harmonic information.

I can only deal with these frequencies using a shelving filter to reduce the low frequencies, and then, when printed back into the DAW, I will use a high-pass filter to reduce them further. Sharp cuts via a minimal phase filter will introduce resonance and phase at lower frequencies. I avoid a linear phase EQ here because it tends to ring when applied at extreme ranges.

Shelving and Baxandall EQs, also called shelving EQs, permit you to attenuate or boost the frequency spectrum's high and low end. They have two parameters: the knee frequency and the boost or attenuation parameter of the frequencies above the knee frequency.

A high shelf attenuates or increases the high frequencies, while a low shelf attenuates or increases the low frequencies. A Baxandall EQ is preferred due to its gentle rising and falling slopes, which exhibit a natural musical sound. The phase shift is spread over a wider area than a conventional parametric shelf, so it is a popular tool when mastering.

I commonly find myself reducing higher and lower frequencies with a shelving EQ. Often, electronic dance music submitted for mastering exhibits too much high-frequency detail and the low frequencies will be entirely out of control. This is because many speaker monitors and environments cannot accurately represent music's lower and higher frequency elements.

I would not advocate using a linear phase EQ for any of these duties because the ringing becomes far more apparent when working at the extremes of the frequency ranges. Therefore, if you have to use a minimal phase to high-pass low frequencies artificially boosted via a shelf, it can introduce phasing on the longer waveforms, resulting in the bass losing cohesion.

Using good EQs when modifying the low and high frequencies is also essential. These are susceptible areas and can suffer from various problems in the digital domain, such as phasing, aliasing, and frequency cramping. This is why I prefer to use hardware, as there is no Nyquist, and the antialiasing filters on the A/D converters ensure no problems.

Chapter 9
Mastering Compression

Compression is perhaps the most overused, abused, and musically damaging processor ever devised. Well, maybe it isn't that severe, but compression is certainly abused in mastering, usually resulting in music that pumps incoherently or sounds flat and bland.

Part of the problem is that compression is difficult to hear if you have underdeveloped listening skills, so it's tempting to go harder than you should. However, overzealous compression will introduce numerous unwanted side effects, particularly on stereo material. Furthermore, it is important to use a specialised mastering compressor rather than a random compressor because throwing *any* compressor across the stereo bus will cause more problems than it solves.

As this is a book on mastering, which comes after production, I will assume the readers know what a compressor is and how it works. So, here, we will concentrate on why and how we use compression in mastering.

Firstly, we only *sometimes* use compression in mastering; it depends on whether the music requires it or not. While many tutorials and articles suggest we *always* apply compression, this isn't the case at all. I estimate approximately half of the music I have mastered has not been through my mastering compressors, while the other half has.

The problem stems from suggestions that compression increases overall volume. While this is correct, it depends on the context. In mastering, we use limiting, *not* compression, to increase the volume during mastering. If we use compression to increase volume, we can only accomplish it by squashing or sculpting the transients in the mix to

DOI: 10.4324/9781032685229-10

provide more headroom and increase the overall volume. This is not efficient or musical and results in flat and uninspiring music.

Instead, we want to use compression to enhance the music's clarity, detail, or density, add vibrancy, and often, tone. We accomplish this by using the compressor to reshape the transients in the music. However, to use a compressor in this way, we must first decide on the *type* of compressor we want to use because this will determine the tone it imparts onto the music.

- Optical
  These employ a photoresistor that reacts to the incoming signal; the light grows brighter as the signal amplitude increases, increasing the compression. It is a program-dependent unit with soft knee compression that is considered natural and transparent.
  Due to the compression's slower nature, it works well with slower genres of music, smoothing out the audio. If the compressor has a tube output stage (which many optical compressors do), it will slightly thicken the material too. I would not employ an optical compressor on high-tempo music with a fast transient kick, as it rarely reacts fast enough and must be followed by a compressor that reacts more quickly to transient material.
- Tube/Variable MU /Delta-MU
  Tubes are the gain control element, working slightly faster than optical. They often add harmonic distortion to the signal, increasing its musicality and thickening the audio. These can be well-suited to many genres of music, adding a musical glue, but the tone can be too colourful if employed on very dense material, making it appear muddy. Depending on the music, Vari-Mu compressors are considered some of the best for mastering; the SPL Iron is one such compressor.
- FET
  Field-effect transistors (FETs) form the gain control in compressors with a linear range that determines the threshold, so they often don't feature a threshold. They react very fast on transients so that you can capture them on high-tempo music, but they distort readily. They can add a bright presence to the sound with a gritty texture, but I do not feel they are subtle enough to use for mastering.

- PWM compression
  These employ pulse width modulation (PWM), essentially high-frequency pulse rates, to control the audio amplitude. They have a swift reaction time and an immaculate sound. They offer distortion-free, smooth compression that can sound excellent on all forms of music. However, they are very clean compressors that do not add any tone or colouration. Therefore, some users will first use a colourful compressor, usually an opto or Vari-mu, and follow it with a PWM.
- VCA
  VCA use a voltage-controlled amplifier on an integrated circuit (IC) chip. They are similar to the FET compressor but do not distort as readily and offer very high transparency. These incredibly versatile compressors lack tone, though, providing extremely transparent compression. The Shadow Hills mastering compressor consists of an optical compressor fed into a VCA; the optical adds the colouration, and the VCA captures any peaks the optical compressor may miss.

Ideally, only a mastering compressor is suited for mastering work. I wouldn't recommend throwing an LA-2A, 1176, or SSL bus compressor across the mix for mastering duties because they are not designed for the job. Mastering compressors are designed to handle the spectral content across the entire medium with more subtlety and fewer unwanted artefacts than a "universal" compressor.

If I employ compression, it is in the hardware stage of my mastering chain. My tool of choice is the SPL Iron Mastering Compressor. This compressor is a powerhouse of vintage-inspired technology mixed with modern production requirements. It produces a well-balanced, rounded sound with additional tube warmth that can add plenty of vibrancy to a mix. While there are other compressors for mastering, such as the Shadow Hills, I don't feel it has a modern enough sound for EDM. I'm sure many would disagree, but this is an industry of opinions, and as they are both available as plug-ins, you can always demo each and see which suits your music and ear.

Compression always starts with actively *listening* to the material you're about to compress and thinking carefully about what you want to achieve. Professionals do not insert processors and then randomly change parameters, hoping to hear something good eventually. If you take this attitude, you will likely apply compression solely because of its density, not whether it serves the music in a positive light.

When listening to the material, we identify what is needed and whether compression can achieve it.

There are generally four reasons we would apply compression during mastering: to tame dynamics, increase the punch, modify the rhythm, or add some glue.

1. Tame dynamics

    The dynamics rarely require taming on a good mix, but the occasional mix may exhibit excessive dynamic behaviour on an instrument. I would usually talk to the mix engineer to see if this could be approached again, but if not, I'd use a compressor to control it.

    When taming dynamics, we listen to instruments that project out at you from the mix. It is essential to differentiate between this occurring due to too much dynamic behaviour or through volume. If we listen to just one note of the instrument (its micro dynamic behaviour), we should judge whether the entirety of the instrument is too loud or its initial attack stage is too hard.

    If it's the latter, we can control it with compression. If it's the former, attempting to fix it with dynamic EQ would be preferable. If the initial attack is too prominent in relation to the instrument, we can use a fast attack setting on the compressor so that every time the peak occurs, the compressor will tame it.

    Notably, the loudest element in a mix is the kick, and we may not want this to drive the compressor, so we may have to use a sidechain so that only the problematic instrument triggers compression.

    A sidechain is when we employ a high-pass filter (HPF) to remove some low-end audio that drives the compressor to react aggressively. Using the sidechain will provide a smoother sound and make the compressor appear more transparent. Many mastering compressors feature side chains that can be switched in.

2. Adding punch

    Electronic dance music relies on its punch. Since the kick will drive the compressor if you use a longer attack time, the kick can creep through unmolested while the energy is captured afterwards. A slightly longer release time will smooth out the power, producing a punchy feel to the music.

The release time must be set carefully, and the compressor must relax before the next kick; otherwise, the whole mix will be captured in the compression cycle, and the attack will no longer perform its desired function.

3. Modify the rhythmic balance or feel.

Often, a mix will benefit from compression on the low-frequency elements, and if compression is applied cautiously, it can improve the relationship between the kick and bass. If you use a short attack setting, the compressor will capture the kick, taming its transient and pulling it closer to the bass. This will make the bass more apparent in the mix. With a short release time, the compressor will relax after the kick, bringing up the bass energy. Both attack and release must be used cautiously, though a too-fast attack time will reduce low-frequency energy, and a too-fast release will cause the mix to pump. If you use a more prolonged attack and release time, the compressor will capture just the bass, removing the kick from the compression cycle.

4. Mix glue

We cannot speak about compression on multiple instruments without discussing mix glue. I have no doubt you used mix glue via parallel compression on the drum bus while mixing, but it also occurs during mastering.

Mix glue results from multiple instruments sharing a similar dynamic movement alongside small amounts of distortion and compression that thicken the sound. For us to determine the differences between sounds in a mix, there must be systematic perceptual differences between them in terms of dynamics and frequency. This is a function of auditory scene analysis.

When we compress the mix during mastering, the compressor will impose a dynamic movement similar to that of all instruments. Since the kick usually drives the compressor, every instrument will move rhythmically with this kick. Moreover, if we run a signal through a non-linear device, such as compression, the amplitude modulation of the compressor will add a series of additional side-band harmonics to the signal, thickening it. These, combined with the compressor action of restricting the transients, bring the sustained energy of the music forward and give the impression of a denser signal.

This must be applied with caution, though; heavy-handed application will increase the signal density. The increased density fills our hearing spectrum, giving us a euphonic experience (eargasm). However, it comes at the expense of signal clarity as the transients are more compressed, and the sustained portions are more present.

To achieve the glue effect, it would be best to use a fast attack time combined with a longer release. The attack should not be so fast that you lose the low-frequency energy, and the release should be brief enough that the compressor can relax before the next kick. It must also not be too short for the mix to pump uncontrollably.

The trick to mastering compression is to use low ratios (2:1 or perhaps 3:1) and then listen carefully to the effects of attack and release times. Attack times will change the relationship of the instruments in the mix; if they are fast, they will increase signal density because the sustained elements of the mix will increase, whereas if they are slow, they will add punch and vibrancy to the music. However, they will remove low-end energy from the mix if they are too fast.

Multiband Compression

We can also apply multiband compression in addition to full-band compression. Compressors such as the Maselec MLA-4, Flux Alchemist, or the APB16 MC-3 allow you to compress over several separate frequency bands.

Various bands provide more flexibility, allowing you to work individually with the track's dynamics. Since the low frequencies will often drive the compressor, you can use a compressor on the low bands, another on the mid bands, and another on the high bands, all without affecting one another.

I only use multiband occasionally when a dynamic imbalance occurs in the mix. For example, bass and kick do not occur only in the low frequencies; they will also extend into the higher frequency ranges. Sometimes, these may create problems such as pumping in the upper mid-range, particularly if the producer has used pumping or volume-shaping tools to modify them.

In this instance, you can even out the mid-bands with light compression, tame the transients with a fast attack, increase the density, and reduce pumping effects. This approach can also be helpful if the mid-bands need more energy, a common problem with many mixes.

As volume increases, the bass and higher frequencies become perceivably louder than the mid-range, which appears to dip in amplitude. Inexperienced producers and mix engineers will emulate this effect without realising it by increasing the amplitude of low and high-frequency instruments. This results in insufficient energy in the mid-band of the music, and therefore, increasing density with compression can help bring them forward.

However, multiband compression must not be treated as a volume control because it affects the material's dynamics. It can cause an imbalance in the tonality, affecting the overall musical ambience. Furthermore, these compressors will introduce phase cancellation at the crossover frequencies of each band that, if it occurs where the fundamental frequencies of an instrument lie (the instrument's pitch), can result in the instrument dropping back in the mix.

This can be particularly problematic with music such as Uplifting trance, as this is a very melodic genre, and the leads and bass change pitch regularly. If the crossover frequency occurs at the fundamental of just one of these melodic shifts, it will move to the back of the mix every time that pitch occurs. This can be easy to miss, so you must pay attention to this happening (Figure 9.1).

Figure 9.1 Our APB-16 MC-3 multiband compressor.

Chapter 10

Mid/Side Processing and Stereo Width

I don't think writing a book on mastering without discussing mid-side would be possible. Over the past 10 years, it has become the buzzword of the audio industry, with many developers releasing plug-ins that offer producers and mastering engineers the option to apply mid-side processing to their work.

Countless videos and online articles show the myriad ways we can use mid-side processing to fix errors in a mix, add excitement, control instruments' behaviour, and apply stereo-widening. It's a magical processor, apparently. Yet, mid-Side processing can destroy a master if you don't know exactly how it works or its application. To understand why, we should first examine stereo and mono.

Many sources suggest that mono is no longer critical because of technological advances. I disagree; music must always be mono-compatible because, unless heard on headphones or EarPods, most of the listening public will first experience your music in mono.

To experience stereo, we must either wear headphones or be positioned in the sweet spot, directly between both speakers and at the proper distance from them. This is usually the same, or similar, distance as the speakers are apart from one another. If you remain in the centre of the speakers but begin to move backwards, away from the speakers, the sound will eventually conform to mono.

Now, consider how often you sit in the sweet spot when you're not producing music. Coffee shops, supermarkets, shopping centres, malls, bars, pubs, clubs, and even the gym rarely use stereo systems because you must be in the sweet spot to experience it properly.

DOI: 10.4324/9781032685229-11

Even driving your car, you are closer to one speaker than the other, and that's not to mention that smart speakers such as Alexa and Apple's Homepod are mono systems, too.

Of course, you may be aiming solely for the clubs, but many clubs are mono, and if stereo, you would only experience it when you're in the sweet spot; any other time, such as the left or right of the club, or at the bar, it will appear in mono. Thus, it's fair to say that mono remains more critical than stereo.

Although this is a book on mastering, to understand the problems with mid-side processing and the difficulties it introduces in mono, we must first discuss some basic mixing principles, such as cardinal mixing. This technique describes panning an instrument to its cardinal position (entirely left or right).

If a mix using this approach were summed to mono, any instrument wholly panned left or right would become 6 dB quieter than every other instrument sitting in the centre of the mix. This is because all central sounds co-exist in both speakers simultaneously and will increase in amplitude when summed together for mono.

$$\text{Left Channel} + \text{Right Channel} = \text{Mono Signal} \left(= +6\text{dB} \right)$$

When the music is summed to mono, any equally present sound in the left and right channels will be 6dB louder. This also means that if a signal only exists in the left or right channel, the signal amplitude is halved when it is summed to mono.

Some confuse this math with the panning law, but this does not affect summing to mono and instead deals with how the instrument's amplitude behaves as you pan from left to right. Under panning law, a sound in one speaker will be quieter than a sound occurring in both, so as you pan from one speaker to the middle, the amplitude will fall to maintain the same volume (as determined by the panning law you use) as both speakers now share the energy.

So, how does this relate to mid-side applications? Mid-side, or, to use its correct term, Sum and Difference, follows a similar principle. It's been around since the 1930s when Alan Blumlein first started experimenting with coincident microphone positioning. It is simply an alternative working method with two audio channels separated via a matrix.

Many view this matrix as a way to work with two mix elements separately. In other words, it permits us to work independently on the mix's mono (mid) and the stereo information (sides). However, with a sum and difference matrix, instruments on the side of the mix will also be present in the centre. To understand why, we must examine the matrix, and at the risk of oversimplifying, it works as follows:

$$Mid = Left + Right$$
$$Side = Left(-Right)$$

What we should note about this matrix is that to subtract the right channel from the left, we invert the polarity of the right channel, permitting us to deduct it from the left. This is why it is called a sum and *difference* matrix. The phase inversion of the right channel creates the difference.

Many confuse this as the complete separation of mono and stereo elements, but this isn't possible. If you have a mix with a hi-hat, for example, panned to the cardinal left of the stereo image and run this through the matrix, the hi-hat will now exist on the sides *and* the mid. This is evident from the math.

$$Mid = L + 0 = L\left(Left + Right\right)$$
$$Sides = L - 0 = L\left(Left - Right\right)$$

Furthermore, if the hi-hat were panned to the right instead, it would still be present in the mids but appear as a polarity-flipped signal on the sides.

$$Mid = 0 + R = R\left(Left + Right\right)$$
$$Side = 0 - (-R) = -R\left(Left(-Right)\right)$$

Therefore, if we apply the processing to only the difference (the sides), and there are instruments panned solely here, we will equally affect them in the centre, which can result in unwanted issues.

Furthermore, because the difference results from phase modification of the matrix, it will affect the mix in stereo if we use any processors that modify the phase of the difference. For example, a standard recommendation is to use EQ to boost the high frequencies at the "sides" of a mix. The theory is that returning to stereo will introduce a stereo-widening effect to the music at the higher frequencies.

However, if a signal is panned to the left and you use a minimal phase EQ, the phase introduced onto the left channel will mix with the non-phase-adjusted signal in the centre when the matrix returns to stereo. In this instance, you would *have* to use a linear phase EQ because any processing that works on the principle of phase will introduce problems in a sum and difference matrix.

Furthermore, you must be cautious that the linear phase EQ does not introduce any ringing artefacts. Otherwise, you may find yourself chasing the resonances that *you've* introduced into the material. Remember the mantra – "do no harm."

Whenever we use any form of mid-side processing, we must consider the signal's phase and how we may affect it. We must also consider the matrix itself and the fact that any adjustments to the mid-channel will affect all instruments regardless of their pan position. Adjustments to the side channels will affect everything except the mono elements in the mix.

I always recommend mono the mix whenever you make any adjustments and listening to how they have affected its compatibility. Then, follow this by isolating the sides and then isolating the mids to hear exactly how you may have affected them. The Voxengo MSED is a free mid-side encoding plug-in that permits you to solo the mid and the sides, while numerous plug-ins are designed for mid-side EQ and compression (Figure 10.1).

I recommend only using mid-side processing if you know exactly how you will affect the audio and have the monitoring environment to hear its effects. Typically, it emphasises instruments or vocals in the mix

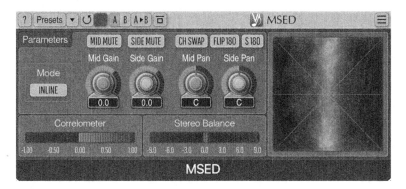

Figure 10.1 The Voxengo MSED mid-side encoder.

during mastering or increases the stereo width. These are accomplished via EQ, compression or harmonic exciters.

For reasons discussed already, you must use a linear phase EQ when using the matrix. The application depends on the material's requirements, but I may typically apply some EQ boosts to the mid-channel, particularly on bass instruments. This will often increase the presence in the mix, creating a more powerful bass signal to sit with the kick.

Alternatively, I may use compression on the mid-signal if the bass doesn't exhibit much density. By compressing with a fast attack time, the compressor will balance the dynamics, creating a more extended sustain period to help make trousers flap in a club.

I may also use an EQ on the sides of the mix by applying wide boosts to leads, vocals, claps, or hi-hats, which increases their stereo presence in the music. This can make them pop out of the mix more, adding excitement.

The general theory behind applying EQ in a mid-side matrix is if you apply a boost to the sides, it will add stereo width, whereas if you use a cut to the sides, it will reduce the stereo width. This also works vice versa when working with just the mid; boosts will reduce the width, and cuts will increase it. It's up to you how you choose to apply it, but as mentioned, you must always check the mix in mono, on sides only and mid only after any modification.

You can also apply harmonic exciters or additional reverberation to the side signals to enhance the music because these will be reduced as soon as the matrix returns to stereo. This is a widespread technique with genres such as uplifting trance; the leads are often swamped in reverb, which sounds great in stereo but turns to mud in mono. Applying some reverb to the leads on just the sides disappears in mono.

While mid-side techniques can enhance the stereo width of recordings, an alternative way to introduce this is by changing the phase between the left and right channels with a delay line. Many stereo widening plug-ins will use either mid-side or phase to achieve their effect. These often work by introducing a delay between a stereo mix's left and right channels.

The application is similar to mixing; for example, when mixing guitars, it is common practice to pan them to the left and right of the stereo field and then apply different processing on each. This may be the same guitar amp on both, but using different settings. The more the settings change, the more significant the difference between the left and right channels. We perceive a more expansive space as the channel phase becomes more disparate.

Note, however, that if too much stereo width is applied, we will lose volume when playing the track in mono. This is due to the waveforms on each channel being out of phase, and when combined, some destructive interference cancels the sound.

Another method to create a wider stereo field illusion is via a multiband width processor. I sometimes use a Drawmer 1976 with three independent frequency bands for width processing on each selectable band, which can be adapted depending on the audio material's requirements. iZotope Ozone has a similar multiband feature for harmonic enhancement and stereo widening.

When using these enhancers, frequencies below 100 Hz are best kept mono. In EDM, we want to maintain the punch of the lows, so the lower frequencies of both kick and bass are mono. By doing so, they share the energy from both speakers, which helps them propagate more efficiently. Then, space and the illusion of size and depth can be added to the mid and high frequencies.

As with mid-side processing, however, we must always check for mono compatibility as you work. It is pretty easy to move from having some instruments present to suddenly disappearing when the mix is summed.

Chapter 11
Saturation

The mantra of many mastering engineers is "do no harm". Roughly translated, do not perform any processing to the audio that is not required. This is because one of the first rules of audio engineering is that any processing or effects you apply will have positive and negative consequences.

EQ, for example, will introduce phase shifts; compression will introduce additional harmonics in the form of sidebands; the mid-side can affect the phase of the left and right channels, and numerous plug-ins can introduce aliasing, etc. You get the picture.

Before applying any processing during mastering, we must consider how such processing might affect the audio positively and negatively and weigh the options. Because these effects are most noticeable on complete stereo material, many mastering engineers will avoid applying any processing if possible. This is even more so when applying effects such as harmonic saturation, which is a hot topic among many mastering engineers.

Some engineers believe we should only apply processors to a master, not effects. Employing effects such as saturation often distorts and deliberately damages the audio clarity. Others feel it continuously improves the audio and utilise it all the time, while some will only use it depending on the material.

I feel that as long as what we do to the audio is beneficial, saturation is a tool like any other. If used subtly, it can introduce colour and add warmth and vibrancy to the material. Indeed, many mastering processors, such as the SPL Iron, will add saturation to the material anyway due to its topology. It is a Vari-Mu (tube)compressor, so it will add subtle

DOI: 10.4324/9781032685229-12

Figure 11.1 The Oven plug-in is also available in hardware.

amounts of saturation to the signal. However, you must be cautious about applying saturation directly as a deliberate effect, as it can equally impact the spectral density and balance of the music.

Several plug-ins and hardware can be used to add saturation during mastering. These can be helpful if the processing you use does not add any through its topology. Mastering engineer Maor Appelbaum and HendyAmps created "The Oven," for this purpose. It's a dedicated multiband saturation unit designed for production *and* mastering purposes (Figure 11.1).

Many engineers choose between tube and tape when applying saturation to a master. Although many other forms of saturation exist, including solid-state, the preferred application during mastering is light amounts of tube, tape, or sometimes both.

Tube Saturation

Tube saturators are available as hardware or plugin emulations. Triode tube saturation is often applied to add even harmonics to the audio. These second-order harmonics occur at double the input frequency, a musical integer value that provides more musical results.

Tubes, however, can also add third-order harmonics. These are created via pentode tubes, but these harmonics do not occur at musical integers of the input signal and do not sound as musical, adding more of a harder, punchy edge to the material.

When applying tube saturation, I recommend hardware over software, primarily due to the possibility of introducing aliasing into the signal with a plug-in. As discussed in an earlier chapter, saturation relies on adding harmonics at all frequencies, which can exceed the Nyquist, resulting in aliases appearing in the audible range if the plug-in does not use appropriate filters to reduce or eliminate it.

Even then, elliptic up-sampling, over-sampling, symmetric FIR low-pass filters, and several other methods employed to reduce aliasing can introduce sonic artefacts of their own. These can vary from skewing the signal phase to affecting the transient information or introducing heavy latency issues that can lead to plugin delay compensation (PDC) issues in some DAWs.

All digital audio workstations employ delay compensation for the plug-ins. This is necessary because any form of digital processing takes a finite amount of time to complete. If the workstation does not compensate for this processing time, every time audio passes through a plugin, it will be delayed, resulting in channels running out of time with one another. The plugin, however, must report the correct time required to process the audio because if this is incorrect, it will create problems such as smearing transient behaviour.

These can all have severe consequences when working on a complete mix. Therefore, at the risk of sounding privileged, I recommend being highly cautious about applying tube saturation during mastering unless you can use hardware to accomplish it.

I use a Black Box HG-2 for tube saturation in masters. Two tubes are fitted: triode to generate more musical harmonics and pentode to add aggression to the material. Due to its design, the two saturation types can be mixed and matched via serial or parallel configurations to suit the music genre.

Choosing which to use depends on the material you're working with. I find that genres I consider aggressive and hard-hitting, such as hardstyle, drum and bass and bass house, benefit from the more aggressive pentode distortion, whereas "softer" genres, like house, benefit more from triode distortion.

Tube saturation must, however, be applied with extreme caution because it can damage the music without you realising it. Adding second-order harmonics will thicken the sound, adding density to the signal and making it more appealing to our ears. However, second-order harmonics on lower-frequency instruments often make them less defined, blurring the image and softening their impact.

Figure 11.2 Our Black Box HG-2 is also available in a plugin.

Third-order harmonic distortion works well on lower frequencies, adding punch, weight, and definition, but it can also make higher frequencies sound abrasive and brittle. This can be particularly noticeable on vocals, leads and hi-hats.

Therefore, when mastering, applying saturation is a balancing act that requires careful listening and gentle application. It is an effect that should be used so that you feel something is missing when it's not present, but you don't notice it when it *is* present.

Furthermore, if you use any tube equipment for mastering, you must keep up with their maintenance by replacing the tubes as they age. Tubes will introduce resonance, ringing and crackling as they wear, and this can be so subtle it's unnoticeable unless you pay attention. You could be damaging the material without even noticing (Figure 11.2).

Tape Saturation

Adding the harmonic saturation from tape has become fashionable in mastering, and many plugins are designed to emulate it. While you could use a hardware tape machine, finding one may be something of a challenge. You can't use your Sony Walkman; it must be a tape machine designed for studios. These are large, bulky, and incredibly expensive to maintain and purchase, so a plug-in is likely the only viable option. Of course, this raises the question of aliasing problems from a plug-in, but there are some workarounds to this that we will discuss later.

Tape emulation will add third-order harmonic distortion to the material alongside several other "effects", depending on how it is configured and the model used. Many online sources recommend using a faster tape speed of 30 inches per second (IPS) during mastering, but it depends on the genre.

30 IPS will maintain high-frequency detail but it comes at the cost of low-frequency definition, while a slower speed (15 IPS) will increase the definition of lower frequencies, but this comes at the expense of

Figure 11.3 The UAD Studer tape plug-in.

high-frequency detail. Some genres, such as Tech House, rely more on low-frequency content than high, so I suggest a slower tape speed. However, a higher tape speed is more appropriate for genres such as Uplifting Trance, as the energy is in the leads. Furthermore, the material's transient behaviour must also be considered because of tape hysteresis.

As the tape passes the recording head, it takes a finite amount of time for the oxide particles on the tape to absorb and release the magnetism. If a transient passes the recording head too quickly, its amplitude will skew, reducing its impact.

Some plug-in emulations permit you to increase (or decrease) this hysteresis effect via the tape bias, acting in some ways similar to a transient designer. Low bias settings will harden transients and increase brightness but may also add minor distortion to the mid frequencies. A higher setting will smear transients and gently roll off the higher frequencies. Using tape in this way can help glue a mix together without the side effects of compression.

If the tape is driven hard, it will also saturate, but the effects will depend on how hard it is driven. When only slightly overdriven, the transients will soften, resulting in a slight compression effect, whereas the more the input signal is increased, the lower frequencies will exhibit odd harmonic distortion. This increases the punch and presence of low frequencies, but it comes at the expense of losing the higher frequencies and compressing the signal.

Multi-band Saturation

A multi-band tape or harmonic saturation unit would be the most obvious solution to the problems we may experience using tape and tubes. Low frequencies could benefit from the added depth of third-order harmonic saturation, helping glue the instruments together and increasing punch and vibrancy.

Most synths are digital or plug-in with EDM; saturation can help bring them to life and sound more natural. Second-order harmonic distortion could be used to tame and smooth high frequencies. The subtle taming of transients and the musical nature of the saturation may add thickness and warmth to these, making the music appear smoother.

Figure 11.4 The Drawmer 1976 Stereo three band saturation and width processor.

This was the idea behind Maor Appelbaum's The Oven, but many other hardware units can achieve the same. The Drawmer 1976 has three bands with adjustable cross-over frequencies. It provides the control to add presence and grit to the lows and then smooth out the highs without affecting the punch of the lows (Figure 11.4).

Of course, several multi-band saturation plugins are on the market that could be used. Fabfilters Saturn or United Plugins Plamen allow you to select a different amount of saturation for several bands. However, while applying the third order at lower bands is unlikely to create aliasing, the second order at higher bands may, so this must be used cautiously.

Moreover, the multiband application of any processor or effect requires filters to separate the bands. All filters will introduce phase, the extent of which depends on the filter's design. Beyond the phase affecting the material, if the crossover frequency occurs at the same point as a fundamental frequency (which determines the pitch), it will disappear into the mix every time this note appears.

This returns us to the beginning of the chapter; we must always weigh how our processing will affect the audio. Because these effects are most noticeable on complete stereo material, we should ideally avoid applying any processing if possible.

Chapter 12
Limiting

Enter any discussion on mastering, and limiters are the number one subject. Many consider these the definitive tools for mastering music because they're ultimately responsible for making your music loud.

Although this is not always the case, limiting is the nevertheless the processor you apply to your mastering chain. However, once you know more about limiting and how it can be employed, you will likely be tempted, like I was, to introduce more than just one brick-wall limiter at the end of your mastering chain.

Many articles will suggest that a compressor with a high ratio above 20:1 is a limiter, but this isn't accurate. Compressors feature a ratio to make them more of a musical tool by permitting some of the signal to exceed the threshold. A limiter has no ratio and will always prevent a signal from exceeding the threshold. Therefore, even if a compressor is set with a ratio of 20:1, the sound will still exceed the threshold and, thus, cannot perform as a limiter.

Many believe the first limiter was the LA-2A, designed in the 1960s, but again, this isn't accurate. The first peak limiters were designed for broadcasting and used in the 1930s. The first commercial peak limiters were by Western Electric and RCA in 1937, soon followed in the mid-1940s by a Langevin ProGar 119A Program Guardian tube limiter/compressor.

Despite the commercial use of these limiters for many years, the infamous LA-2A, invented in the early 1960s by James F Lawrence, reaps the most attention. The LA2A was an optical, tube-based compressor to manage the dynamics, and although it was marketed as a limiting amplifier, it was not a limiter in the strictest sense.

DOI: 10.4324/9781032685229-13

Indeed, even the 1176 Peak Limiter that followed in 1976 was not a limiter but a dynamic range compressor. Perhaps bizarrely, the first brick wall limiter was in *software*: the Waves L1 Ultramaximiser, released in 1994, which is also credited with starting the loudness wars.

The introduction of compact discs released mastering engineers from the limitations of vinyl, offering a higher dynamic range with a higher bandwidth. This meant that engineers could increase the volume of mixes, and as we perceive louder to sound better, the Waves L1 limiters were abused. Engineers would push their limiters to the absolute maximum, sacrificing dynamics in return for loudness.

But even that wasn't enough; once mastering engineers had pushed limiters as far as possible, they would deliberately clip their analogue to digital converters when printing the signal back into the DAW to make the music sound even louder.

This "clipping" loudness was a result of saturation clipping. Chopping the top off a signal's transients makes it more like a square wave. This process introduces further third-order harmonics, giving the impression that the music is harder and louder. This process was considered a more transparent form of limiting because there are no attack and release times to cause unwanted pumping.

While several efforts have been made to prevent the loudness wars, the success of individuals such as Ian Shepherd is questionable at best. The engineers who want to end the loudness wars believe they have succeeded following announcements that streaming platforms are increasing or decreasing the music volume. However, this is more about ensuring that the listening audience does not experience sudden changes in amplitude while streaming music than maintaining musical dynamics.

While music played at lower volumes will always sound better with its musical dynamics intact, the loudness war is still ongoing. The only difference is that it now occurs behind closed doors in bedroom studios, on the fringes of music production. It's promoted by those who don't know any better and think loudness is the be-all and end-all of music. This is no surprise, though. Mastering is the final stage before release and should be delivered to a third person to perform a final quality check. We cannot quality-check our own work; therefore, if we choose to master our own music, all we are left with is loudness.

When I master a record, I want to ensure the master is loud but not so much that I sacrifice the dynamics. Even then, for some, this is still "not loud enough," and they request it to be louder. Until that is, they hear their release on Apple Music or Spotify months later and email to ask why it sounds so awful on streaming services.

I do not believe in mastering as loud as possible because it is still a widely misunderstood perception. The human ear is complex; it's a combination of frequency and duration that affects our perception. Indeed, loudness can be as related to the production process as it can be with mastering.

Sounds of a longer duration will appear louder than peak signals, even at the same amplitude. So, if music consists mainly of transient, peak material, it will not be perceived as loud as material that exhibits more sustained sounds. This means we cannot simply measure and copy the LUFS value from another artist's music. If their music exhibits more sustained periods from their production process, it will sound louder at a lower LUFS value.

Furthermore, despite LUFS being closer to how we perceive loudness, it is not entirely accurate, and production methods will change its relative value. We should never attempt to crush the life out of a piece of music just because we want to match some arbitrary LUFS value.

As discussed previously, EDM must exhibit dynamics to maintain punch; otherwise, the kick will be lost in the music. Streaming services employ a loudness normalisation process that automatically adjusts a track's playback volume. This isn't a form of limiting; it's an amplitude control, turning down the volume of any music that is too loud and turning up music too quiet to prevent sudden volume changes between tracks.

Furthermore, today's DJ mixers are pretty advanced, featuring a volume control for both decks. Serious DJs, those who love the music more than themselves and spend more time mixing music than waving their hands around, are well aware of this feature.

There is no need to crush the audio, and it is far better to be a little more relaxed with the limiter to maintain the punch and vibrancy of the music so it sounds good on all systems. This is the very essence of mastering.

Limiter Control

Limiters are relatively simple, usually consisting of three parameters: a threshold, an output ceiling, and a release parameter. The threshold is like a compressor and defines the level at which the limiter will begin its processing. Any signals that would typically exceed the threshold will reduce in gain to the level determined by the output ceiling.

The standard output ceiling is 0 dBFS, which is the extreme limit of a digital system. If you exceed this, the signal will distort when it is bounced. However, unless the limiter is true peak and shows no signal distortion, I strongly advise setting the output ceiling to -0.5 or -1 dBFS.

Limiters can offer one of two measurements: the current peak loudness or the true peak loudness. True peak is the preferred metering because it takes the digital-to-analogue conversion process into account. The signal may exceed a peak value after conversion due to the D/A conversion process "rounding off" the bits.

If you recall in an earlier chapter, signal magnitude is stored as bits in a digital system. When these are converted into an analogue audio waveform, there is often a variation in level, with the analogue waveform becoming slightly above the maximum digital value. This can result in distortion of the signal on the peaks (Figure 12.1).

These "inter-sample" peaks aren't always noticeable, and as music will typically be clipped by the mastering engineer, the additional harmonic distortions introduced by this method will disguise them. However, they mustn't occur for broadcast, so it is worth always working to one standard: the best. We become what we practice, so ensuring that we do not have any inter-sample peaks is the best approach.

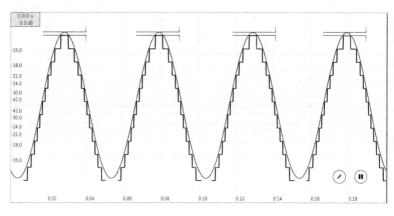

Figure 12.1 Notice the "additional information" added to the very top of the digital waveform on conversion.

In theory, we should use true peak limiters, which offer true peak metering and leave some headroom above the current output ceiling to cater to the conversion process. However, many of these will compromise the transient detail, and I prefer to use true peak metering rather than true peak limiting.

I recommend setting the output ceiling to a maximum of - 0.5 dBFS, and I often configure my ceiling to - 1 dBFS. This is because some stereo-widening processes, particularly those that rely on phase to accomplish the effect, can fool limiters into providing a false reading that results in distortion when bounced. Furthermore, on conversion to AAC or MP3, signals bounced at 0 dBFS can cause overload distortion on these compression formats.

The release time on a limiter must also be set cautiously. This determines the time it takes for the limiter to relax when the output signal falls below the input (like compression, the release on limiters does *not* monitor the threshold).

On most EDM material, the kick will trigger the limiter, and if the release time is too fast, it can result in audible pumping and distortion. If it is too slow, the limiter will not recover for the next kick, distorting further transients. Many limiters now feature an auto-release, and it's best to use these because they use psychoacoustic modelling to determine the changing release times to minimise distortion.

Some limiters also feature a knee, but whether you can adjust this depends on the limiter. Knees are employed because an immediate attack value may create clicks or distortion as it clamps down on the transients. With a knee, a smoother curve for 10 or 15 milliseconds prevents unwanted clicks. This is the principle behind an ultra-maximiser.

Stacking Limiters

While you can employ one limiter at the end of your signal chain, I prefer to use several, one after the other, to limit the signal gradually. By massaging the signal this way, I can add the sonic character of limiters while also maintaining an open soundstage with less damage to the transients, which are often compromised with just one limiter set to stun.

Remember that limiting is a form of compression; there is always a sweet spot. If you set your limiter to stun (limit the signal hard) and listen carefully as you slowly dial it back – even though limiting is still occurring – you will hear the audio soundstage return. We should apply the right amount of limiting to comply with streaming standards, but it is equally important that you listen to how the audio is affected.

This limiter can then be followed with another, different limiter, following the same procedure. Working in this way, each adds to your overall sound, maintaining sonic integrity and adding colour and thickness. Using several instead of just one also means manipulating the audio gently so the results are more pleasing.

I have access to 4 analogue limiters, each with different quirks and values, bringing different quantities to the final sonic sound. While I use hardware, there are software emulations of each. I don't necessarily use all of these limiters during a master; I may use only a couple, and I may use them in different orders, but each adds a character that the music may or may not benefit from.

I sometimes begin with a Chandler Limited TG 12413 Zener Limiter Stereo Compressor/Limiter, a discrete studio limiter based on a vintage electric and musical industries (EMI) circuit used on The Beatles and Pink Floyd. This limiter introduces a weighty "thickness" to the material, a light vintage warming effect that makes the music appear more forward (Figure 12.2).

I might follow this with a Looptrotter Emperor limiter, which can be used as a compressor, limiter, or harmonic distortion generator. It is a

Figure 12.2 The TG12413 limiter.

Figure 12.3 The Looptrotter Emperor.

reasonably creative device that adds warmth, brightens the audio, and increases perceived loudness. It enables you to control the wet and dry signal to decide how much of the signal is preserved, which is essential when maintaining the audio signal's dynamics (Figure 12.3).

I usually always employ a Bettermaker Mastering limiter. This is digitally controlled analogue hardware. This has many features, including mid/side processing and the option to emulate clipping A/D converters to add further volume. These can be applied as third-order harmonic and second-order harmonic distortions. More on these in a moment (Figure 12.4).

Figure 12.4 The Bettermaker Mastering limiter.

Figure 12.5 The APB16 L-18.

When the material is recorded back into the box, I often use a McDSP APB16 L-18 limiter. This analogue limiter is controlled via a software plugin that can be transparent. If you choose, you can add colour by subtly saturating the higher frequencies, adding vibrancy to the top end of a mix (Figure 12.5).

The final stage is to place a pure software limiter across the material. This is for little more than brick wall security. I use the Fabfilter Pro-L 2 for this process. As mentioned, when setting the true peak, I use -1 dB TP to ensure no distortion occurs when conversion or encoding occurs (Figure 12.6).

As mentioned, I only sometimes use all the limiters; I will mix and match them to provide the best results for the material. Often, a

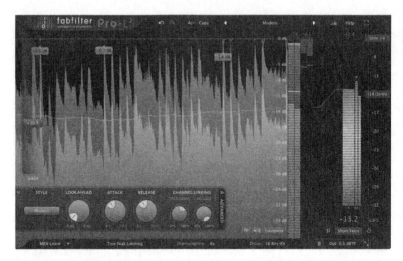

Figure 12.6 Fabfilter Pro L2.

mastering engineer will be limited by the tools they have at their disposal or their knowledge of that plugin or hardware.

We can compare this to being a chef. To the novice chef, a bread knife might appear similar to a carving knife; to an experienced chef, though, who has a whole selection of knives to choose from, they will know that each knife is suited to a specific task.

The same is essential for a mastering engineer, so to have only one limiter that you apply at the end of your chain is an ill-educated attitude. Audio must be sliced like vegetables or protein, sometimes with gentle cuts and sometimes more significant determined hacks. So, if you intend to master it, I recommend growing your toolset.

Moreover, not all genres are the same, and you cannot treat rock music like classical or EDM. Audio does not always fit some preconceived pigeonhole. The client might send in a track they describe as drum and bass, but it might contain slightly different sonic values when I listen. Therefore, it cannot be treated as a generic drum and bass.

Clipping

As mentioned, some limiters allow the application of colour via clipping. Adding this can make audio perceivably louder without the compression artefacts we may receive from heavy limiting. Depending on the limiter, we can add two forms of colour during the mastering process: saturation or distortion.

Saturation is the addition of extra harmonics to the audio, usually occurring at musical integers. This makes the sound appear warmer, thicker, and smoother. The application of tubes provides us with this warm saturation sound and is a technique more suited to higher frequencies than lower ones. If we apply too much saturation to lower frequencies, the thickness can result in muddying of the signal. However, it will thicken the sound at higher frequencies of 1 kHz and above while maintaining clarity.

Distortion occurs when additional harmonics occur at non-integer values. These harmonics develop via peak distortion in mastering due to peak clipping. If we take a sine wave and drive it hard into a converter, it will transform into a square wave as the top of the sinusoidal wave is crushed or removed. This action is shown in Figure 12.7.

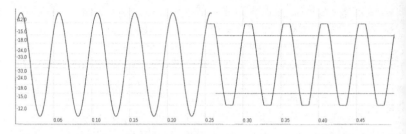

Figure 12.7 In clipping, the top of the waveform is sliced off, converting the waveform to a square.

Modifying a waveform is known as wave shaping. Removing the top of a waveform via clipping adds odd-order harmonics, which add an aggressive nature to the music. This can work particularly well for enhancing the lower-frequency energy but can become destructive if applied too heavily to higher frequencies.

Distortion applied in this way will increase our perception of volume due to adding further harmonics, but if used too heavily, it will harm the music. Clipping in analogue is typically smoother than in the digital realm. The action is less sharp than digital, producing a softer, more controlled sound. However, note that clipping will always compress the sound further, whether in digital or analogue, and we must constantly work to maintain a crest factor to ensure punch in the music.

Chapter 13
Metering

While we require a reliable monitoring chain and trained ears to master, we must also rely on some metering tools to inform us of the loudness and any problems that may be difficult to perceive via monitors or headphones, regardless of their accuracy. For this chapter, we'll examine the various metering tools that are essential to any mastering engineer.

The first meter I rely on is a vector scope, which features a goniometer and a correlation meter. Using a fake phosphor-type effect, the goniometer displays a mix's stereo coherence alongside the stereo panning and dynamics of the music.

The stereo signal is plotted as a two-dimensional graph on two axes, showing the phase correlation. The "shape" of the display indicates this phase coherency. The vertical axis represents the sum of the channels, while the horizontal axis represents the difference. When viewing a mix, the vertical line will, therefore, show signals that are completely in phase with one another, and the further signals are away from this, the more they are out of phase. These effects are shown in Figure 13.1.

When a mix is in stereo, the phosphor effect represents the energy of the mix. In Figure 13.1, for example, a proportionate amount of energy is in the mix's centre, showing that both speakers share the power equally. The stereo elements on the horizontal axis are softer, displayed via a phosphor effect revealing the out-of-phase stereo information. Still, these are quieter as they are not as intense as the vertical.

DOI: 10.4324/9781032685229-14

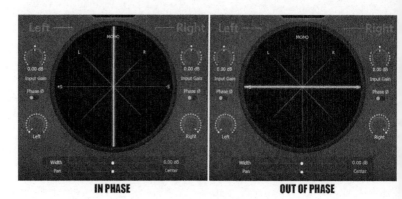

IN PHASE   **OUT OF PHASE**

Figure 13.1 A Goniometer in phase and out of phase.

Using this scope, we can determine several things about the mix:

1. You can determine if the mix is central.
    Some set-ups, particularly if the hardware or DAW has been poorly configured or there is a faulty cable, will result in the mix leaning to the left or right. Typically, the vertical line should be the strongest because most musical elements should remain in phase to translate into mono coherently. Therefore, if this centre vertical line tilts either to the right or left, you can see that the mix is leaning towards one side or the other. In the stereo meter tool, you can adjust the volume or panning of the left or right channel to ensure it sits centrally (Figure 13.2).

    Mono compatibility is essential for all music. While presenters and articles argue that everything is stereo and mono compatibility is unnecessary, I disagree. Many club systems are still mono, and Amazon has sold over half a billion Alexa smart speakers, which are all mono. Moreover, Apple sold over 13 million HomePod systems in 2023, all mono. Considering that many people listen to these smart speakers while cooking, cleaning, or relaxing at home, not ensuring the music is compatible with mono significantly reduces its appeal.

2. You can determine if the mix is too heavily restricted via distortion or clipping.
    The vertical measurement also determines the dynamic restriction via clipping or distortion (wave shaping). If distortion or clipping

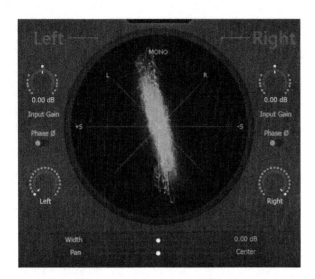

Figure 13.2 A Goniometer showing a mix leaning to the left-hand side slightly.

occurs, the top and bottom of the vertical axis will change into arrows. A mix delivered for mastering should not exhibit this behaviour; otherwise, you will have no dynamic range to work with, and the file may exhibit distortion. If you monitor a mix and cannot hear this but see it, you should return the mix to the delivery engineer (Figure 13.3).

3. You can see the stereo information in the music.
   A glance at the goniometer will inform you of the stereo information contained in the mix. The phosphor dots will indicate the direction and density of the stereo field; the denser the dots, the more data is contained in that area. There is very little stereo information if the mix consists mainly of a single vertical line, and there is too much stereo information if the dots are denser across the horizontal axis than the vertical. Typically, a mix should exhibit a thick vertical line with less density of dots occurring on either side (Figure 13.4).
4. You can see any stereo imbalance.
   The farther the false-phosphor dots move out to the left and right, the further the information is panned in the field. An extensive collection of these dots on either the left *or* right signifies a large amount of stereo information on just one side of the mix, which may cause problems.

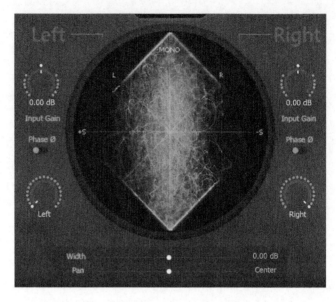

Figure 13.3 A Goniometer showing intense dynamic restriction via distortion.

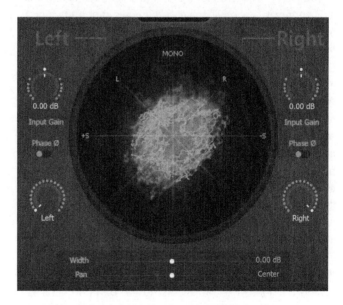

Figure 13.4 A Goniometer showing the stereo information.

Remember that we do not always have access to stereo speakers in many environments. For example, if the drinks bar is on one side of the room or in a gym, you may find yourself over one side of the room for one exercise and then the other for another. If you are driving a car, you are positioned closer to one speaker than the other.

These are all important considerations because if the majority of the stereo signal is occurring in the speaker away from you, you'll only receive half the signal, which could make the music appear lacking. Moreover, any sounds panned entirely to the left or right of an image will halve in volume when the signal is heard in mono (Figure 13.5).

5. You can see polarity and phase issues.

Signals to the left or right of the vertical line determine the panning of instruments. Still, if they occur *above* or *below* the horizontal centre line, the signal is out of phase or polarity.

Almost all vector scopes will feature a correlation meter alongside the goniometer. This informs us of the correlation between the left and right channels. It's usually displayed as a horizontal bar, marked as +1 on the right side, zero in the middle, and -1 on the left. This is shown in Figure 13.6.

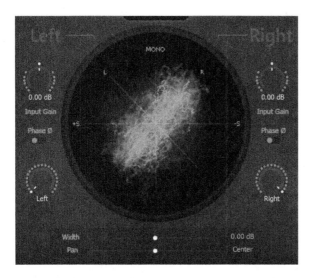

Figure 13.5 The mix is central, but stereo widening has caused an imbalance.

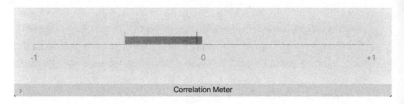

Figure 13.6 A phase correlation meter shows problems with the phase.

The meter displays the phase relation between the left and right channels, showing if there is mono compatibility. If the left and right signals are correlated (i.e., identical), then the meter will be at +1; however, as the phase changes between the left and right channels, it will reduce towards -1. When monitoring a mix, the meter should always fluctuate between zero and +1; if the meter moves beyond this towards -1, then there are phase issues in the mix that will affect its mono compatibility.

Generally speaking, occasionally, the meter moving into the -1 isn't a cause for concern because minor deviations shouldn't negatively affect the mix. However, alongside this metering, I always advise you to mono the mix and listen back cautiously to confirm everything is as it should be. I accomplish this via my monitor controller, but many software plug-ins can be placed on the stereo bus of the mixer to mono the output.

Fast Fourier Transform (FFT)

Many metering plug-ins designed for mastering will feature an FFT meter to monitor the frequency content of the music. These convert time into frequency, but they must be configured correctly and, due to their resolution, are rarely suitable for monitoring lower frequencies with any degree of accuracy.

This is because an FFT is similar in some respects to a movie film. It takes several audio frequency and amplitude snapshots and displays them one after the other to represent a moving image of the frequency bands. However, it can only accurately display frequencies that complete their cycle within the time it has available to measure them. You could compare this measurement to the exposure of a camera.

The lower the frequency, the longer the waveform takes to complete a cycle. If the FFT measurement time, known as a window, is only short

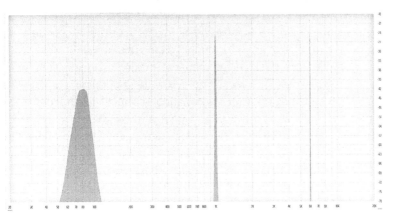

Figure 13.7 The same sine wave test tone occurs at 6 kHz, 1 kHz, and 80 Hz, showing the signal resolution of an FFT reducing as we reach lower frequencies.

(such as 256), it does not have enough time to measure the low-frequency cycles, and, therefore, they are not accurately represented.

Indeed, accurately representing the low-frequency music content requires a window of 16,384; at this setting, each window would be 350 milliseconds, refreshing less than three times per second. This results in a slow-moving FFT, and the number of frequencies that will change in music throughout 350 milliseconds would be significant.

You can test this using a synthesiser or tone oscillator set to a sine wave. If you put the FFT to 2048 samples and play the sine wave at 6 kHz, you can see the accuracy of the measurement – showing a single thin measurement of the fundamental frequency. As you tune the sine wave to lower frequencies, note how the resolution gradually worsens (Figure 13.7).

Consequently, an FFT can be helpful as a casual reference, but it should only be relied on partially. You must trust your ears (and your monitoring environment).

VU Meters

Although you may not think you need to use a VU meter if you're working entirely in the box for your mastering, you should employ one. Many mastering plug-ins are designed to add the harmonic saturation you experience from audio hardware, which reacts differently depending on input gain. If a plug-in is intended to imitate hardware accurately, its behaviour will also change depending on the input level.

VU meters are designed to measure the input signals from inter-connected devices. They let us know if the input or output signal is too "hot". Most analogue hardware is designed to work at its optimum when it receives 0 VU at its input; if the signal is hotter than this, the hard-ware will behave differently, often adding saturation or distortion to the results.

Many plugins are designed to work optimally at the equivalent 0 VU in the DAW, but this is not 0 dBFS; instead, it's approximately -16 to -18 dBFS. You would need to read the operation manual to determine which reference level the developer employs. Regardless, you should ensure that the plug-in receives its signal at the expected level. It will not behave as intended if it exceeds it significantly, and the results can damage the material.

This is why if we are chaining plug-ins together, we must ensure that the output of one plug-in does not overdrive the input of the following plug-in in the chain. For example, if you're using an EQ to boost the signal, this will increase the signal gain at the output of the EQ, which may overdrive the input of the next device in the chain. By placing a software VU meter between the plug-ins, you can determine the gain entering the next in the chain and ensure that it is not being overdriven (Figure 13.8).

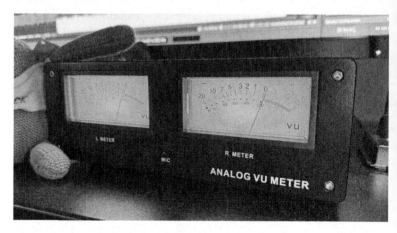

Figure 13.8 The VU meter.

Spectral Balance

I've mentioned spectral balance, or ambience, several times throughout this book because it plays an essential role in mastering. We must
always ensure that the balance and weight of the frequencies along the
spectrum match the genre of music we are mastering. If not, the music
will sound unbalanced.

For example, music with too little bass will sound weak, and music
with excessive highs will sound brittle. More importantly, due to the
nature of our hearing and how the frequency balance changes with
volume, a lot of music will lack the midrange frequencies, yet this is
where the primary energy of music resides.

The spectral balance should ideally be evaluated with only our ears
because we can only sometimes trust what we see. However, if you are
inexperienced at listening, there are plug-ins to help you visualise the
balance of the music. These analyse the music and display the tonal
balance of the music. Using these, you can set the genre and ensure
that any processing you apply maintains the correct spectral balance
(Figure 13.9).

While these are helpful visual aids, they are not specific to genre.
For example, you can choose between jazz, pop, R&B, and electronic
dance music, but you cannot select particular genres within these. This
can make them unreliable, particularly when working with genres such
as Tech House or Drum and Bass, where the music has a very specific
ambience.

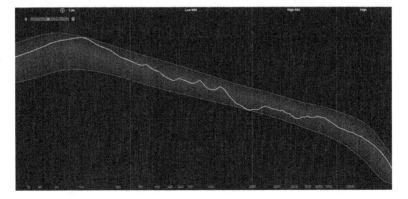

Figure 13.9 The spectral balance.

Furthermore, you may notice instances where it appears as though the balance is incorrect, missing the midrange or some of the highs, but this may be the required balance for that piece of music. If an instrument doesn't exist in the midrange, the meter will show it is lacking in that area, and it can persuade you to apply more correction here when it is not required. This is why these meters, while helpful, should not replace your ears.

LUFS, PLR, PSR, True Peak, and Encoding Metering

The final metering we use for mastering measures loudness, and it often features several measurements, including the integrated LUFS, the momentary LUFS, PLR, and PSR, the true peak measurement, and, sometimes, even how it will sound when encoded.

The number of features depends on the plug-in, but most will include all these. I use Plug-in Alliance Streamliner, as shown in Figure 13.10. All these measurements have already been discussed in detail earlier in this book.

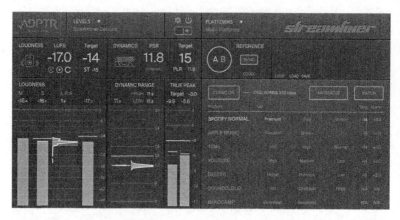

Figure 13.10 ADPTR streamliner.

Chapter 14
Mastering Low Frequencies

Now we have discussed all the processing involved in mastering; we should examine a typical approach to mastering music. When I master a record, I like to listen to music in three frequency bands: the low band, the mid-band, and the high band., and I deal with each accordingly.

Of course, I listen to the effect on all other bands while applying processing or correction on each. However, it is essential to ensure that each band translates accurately; we can begin with perhaps the most difficult– the low frequencies.

Bass is the driving force of EDM. We all want to experience the punch in the chest from a thudding kick and the vibrations of the bass frequencies rattling our teeth and flapping our trousers in a club environment. This low-frequency energy also attracts people outside a club, drawing them in, which every DJ wants because it's how they earn their wages.

Yet, while we love bass-heavy tracks, it's only on the condition that the bass in the record is solid, clear, upright, and forward. Nothing turns the DJ or listeners off more than a flabby bass that is too excessive or entirely out of control. Not only does it sound terrible through a club system, but the DJ has to fight with his deck EQ to control it, and it will heavily affect the punch and groove of the music. DJs will *not* play a track that nobody will dance to because it sounds awful.

Yet, countless producers ignore this fact. They believe they should be able to reliably hear the bass on small monitors in an untreated room; if not, they'll rely on an FFT to tell them what's wrong. So, even though they're working with something they cannot hear or see

DOI: 10.4324/9781032685229-15

accurately, they still expect it to work well in the club, only to wonder why they are struggling to be noticed.

As discussed in previous chapters, many online sources suggest using an FFT to correct errors in low frequencies you cannot hear accurately. However, an FFT does not provide much accuracy at lower frequencies. Even if it did, we cannot seriously expect to be able to work with sound using nothing but our eyes.

As bass frequencies are the longest waveforms, they're the most difficult to propagate for any speaker system. Sub-bass occurs around 20 Hz to 60 Hz, and the bass occurs from 60 Hz to 2 kHz. Sub-bass frequencies are often so low that they are felt rather than heard, while the bass itself can also take up a significant amount of space in a mix. Many near-field monitors cannot propagate these frequencies with a high degree of accuracy.

As discussed previously, a monitor's driver size will determine the frequency's maximum amplitude, shown by the sound intensity = energy/time * area formula. This is a common problem with monitors that consist of smaller drivers or two-way systems, which only have one driver to deal with low-bass *and* mid-range.

We must also consider how bass frequencies are affected by ports and passive radiator systems on monitors. Passive radiator systems are sometimes called drone cones; they don't have a magnet or wire coil but use the sound pressure trapped in the speaker enclosure to recreate a deep bass. Similarly, ported speakers use holes in the speaker's cabinet to enhance bass frequencies. Still, both these approaches create time-dominance effects that smear the bass signal, creating a series of peaks and dips in the low-frequency response. Of course, this is not to mention how your room will affect these longer waveforms if they do propagate.

This is not to suggest that everything you do must be sent to a mastering engineer, but rather to understand your work limitations. Considering that bass is a fundamental element of your music, particularly in EDM, we must ensure it is correct, and that means we *must* be able to hear it accurately. It dictates the groove and low-frequency content and sells the record to the DJ and the clubbers. If we cannot hear it, we cannot work with it, so we cannot act surprised if the music doesn't get anywhere because it translates so poorly on a club system.

Many producers believe that when discussing these problems, we mean the extremely low frequencies that can *"just be removed with some brick wall (a 96dB slope) EQ,"* but this isn't the case. While I expect to experience too much sub-energy in most music delivered to me for mastering, much of the problem occurs higher, between *40 and 400 Hz and* not in the sub-range. This cannot be treated with a "brick wall" EQ.

Many monitoring systems cannot accurately reproduce these frequency bands, leading to poor production decisions and ending with too little or too much energy in this band. The fundamentals of the bass occur here; it is where the kick's lower prominent energy meets the bass and where most of the sideband energy and intermodulation distortion occurs from multiple channels running through non-linear processors.

Furthermore, if the artist has mindlessly followed the typical online advice and articles regarding "ducking" a bass against the kick, there is a cacophony of sideband information that also compromises the clarity of the signal in this frequency band.

In a previous chapter, I discussed the effects of this sidechain ducking; amplitude modulation generates sideband information. For those who skipped it, modifying the amplitude of a signal at speed creates a series of sideband harmonics above and below the affected frequency, as shown in Figure 14.1.

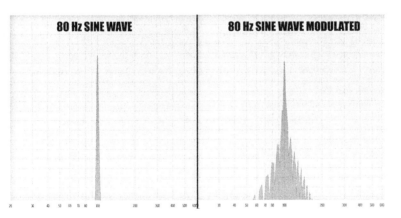

Figure 14.1 The effects of amplitude modulation side-chaining.

This is obviously the effect on a single frequency. Consider how complex a bass signal is, and you can imagine how much unnecessary energy is being introduced into the lower-frequency elements of the mix. I'm not suggesting it should never be used, but rather it should be for good reason beyond "*I can't be bothered to properly learn how to engineer a kick and a bass*."

This *is* a critical area where clarity and definition of a low-end occur, and sometimes mastering cannot solve these problems. I've received many mixes where the bass is so out of control that I cannot correct it, and it has to be returned to the mix engineer. Of course, AI will process it regardless because it's unable to make any knowledgeable or experienced decisions; it'll just imprint an EQ curve and increase the amplitude of the music.

If you do not have the monitoring environment or room, I suggest you ask a professional to master the kick and bass stem while producing the record. You can deliver the kick and bass to a mastering engineer who will ensure the two work together in harmony. I've performed this for many artists and some respectable sample library companies. By doing so, you can create your track, and when it comes to mastering, you don't have to be concerned about low-end clarity.

Techniques for Dealing with Bass Signals

Due to its high energy and low frequency, the kick will trigger a mastering compressor unless we employ a high-pass filter or side chain. However, with EDM, we typically want the kick to drive the compressor because it will introduce a pumping effect to the music (incidentally, this is usually confused with deliberate "ducking" during production).

Attack times must be set carefully to compress a complete mix. If the attack is too fast, the compressor will capture the waveform's initial cycle, reducing its low-frequency content. A slightly longer attack will allow the kick through unmolested, permitting the compressor to work on the bass and instruments afterwards.

The release time will determine the pumping action of the music and the higher-frequency content. If the release time is extended, the higher frequencies will dull slightly as they're captured in the compression cycle. If you shorten the release, these higher frequencies will become more present. If the release is too short, though, it will make the pumping evident and can result in distortion.

It is also important to remember that attack and release can occur multiple times during a single compression cycle. A compressor's release parameter does not monitor the threshold and engages when the input is below its output. A heavy bass signal, therefore, could cause the compressor to track its positive and negative wave states, distorting the compressor if not set appropriately.

You can use multiband compression rather than wideband to control the bass's transient information. However, remember that any multiband system will introduce some phase around the crossover point, so you must ensure it does not negatively affect the material.

You must also be cautious because as the volume of music increases, the mid-range will experience a dip in volume because of how we perceive music. This means it is easy to over-compress the lows because as they're compressed further, the signal density and power will increase, making it appear louder and more appealing to our ears.

If the bass lacks clarity or energy, you could apply some distortion. However, adding distortion or harmonic saturation during mastering can be risky. Beyond the possibility of introducing aliasing artefacts using software, the additional harmonics on longer waveforms can introduce phase issues. This phase can smear the kick and bass's transient response while modifying their timbral character.

Some articles recommend employing mid-side on low frequencies to ensure they are mono, but this matrix can introduce more problems than it solves, particularly on lower frequencies. Instead, I would recommend using a mono plug-in such as Nugen Audio's Mono Filter. With this, you can select a frequency; any occurring below are summed to mono (Figure 14.2).

If the kick or bass requires "tightening" or more transient energy, you can employ EQ, but we must always consider the impact these adjustments may have on other frequency bands. Every action has an equal and opposite reaction in audio, and adjusting one frequency can impact another, such as boosting, cutting or introducing phasing. EQ is a frequency volume control; if we increase or cut one specific frequency, we will affect how the other unaltered frequencies appear.

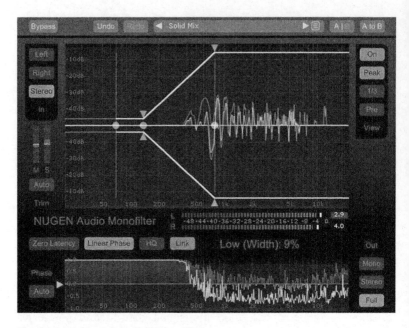

Figure 14.2 Nugen Audio Mono Filter.

I prefer a minimal-phase EQ for the lower frequencies, mainly to remove subfrequencies, because linear-phase EQs usually introduce ringing artefacts. However, it does depend on the EQ you're using, so always try both and listen carefully to the differences each has.

Generally, movements with EQ should always be broad, but as the octave range at frequencies this low is relatively small, you can use higher Q values to pull out elements of the bass or kick to create clarity. I always recommend cutting rather than boosting, however, because boosting any frequency will reduce the available headroom, and when mastering, we can run out of headroom remarkably quickly.

Furthermore, when using a minimal phase EQ, phase distortions will occur around the frequencies being affected, which can result in audible ringing and distortion of the transients. These phase artefacts become more prominent when increasing/boosting frequencies, whereas they become less noticeable when cutting.

We must also be cautious because we can introduce muddiness if we EQ without paying attention. Usually, the 80 to 250 Hz is responsible for a muddy sound, but as the kick and bass often share this frequency range, we must ensure that adjustments do not significantly affect the groove. Additionally, you should take extra care between 100 and 400 Hz because this area contains the energy of the bass. It can be tempting to cut too much here, believing you're adding clarity when, in fact, you're making the track appear anaemic.

I often use a mix of the Charter Oak PEQ-1, API 5500, and the SPL PassEQ. The PEQ-1, in particular, is helpful as it allows you to cut or boost more at frequencies outside the phonlea, producing smoother, more natural results. I follow this with the API, as this EQ is aggressive but has a tonal character and sweetness that can bring out the presence and transients of the bass if they're lacking.

I may also apply a cut of approximately 2 dB at 30 Hz with a boost of 2 dB at 50 Hz with the PassEQ. Due to the EQ's passive nature, this adds a slight frequency bump and colouration at the low end that can work well on many mixes.

Of course, if you do not own this hardware, you may question how to accomplish the same results. This brings us full circle to earlier chapters where I suggested that we know and understand your available tools. You do not require the same hardware I use; many mastering engineers will use different hardware. The real difference is understanding the equipment and how it sounds because only then can you make an informed opinion.

Chapter 15

Mastering Mid-Range Frequencies

The mid-range frequencies are considered to occur between 400 and 6000 Hz. While many online articles suggest that it occurs between 500 and 5000 Hz, they also state that the high range is 6 kHz—20 kHz. This misses a 1000 Hz, so I will refer to the mid-range as 400–6000 Hz.

The mid-range can be subdivided into four frequency ranges: the low, mid, upper mid, and presence range; however, the magic happens at the culmination of these frequencies. This is because the fundamentals and harmonics of nearly all instruments occur within this range. These fundamental frequencies are critical because they define an instrument's pitch. However, if we cannot hear the pitch due to an obscured fundamental, provided we can hear the subsequent harmonics, our brain will fill in the missing information and determine that there must be pitch, and vice versa.

This means we can obscure some of the instrument's harmonics or pitch while mixing but not both. This frequency masking of one or the other often occurs when multiple instruments are mixed, but provided we can hear one *or* the other, we will determine the instrument to be present. This, however, means we must exercise caution during mastering.

A poor choice of EQ, Q value, or frequency to remove resonance can remove a harmonic or fundamental frequency, resulting in an instrument's loss. Furthermore, poor application of multi-band or wide-band compression or saturation can also affect transients and harmonics in the music, changing their balance.

For example, in any multi-band scenario, a poor frequency crossover will result in phase, which may remove fundamentals or harmonics

DOI: 10.4324/9781032685229-16

that are essential to the music. Furthermore, heavy-handed application of wideband saturation could generate harmonics that create negative phase relationships with the signal, or poor compression application could reduce the transient of a fundamental. If this instrument already has its harmonics masked, it could result in losing the instrument.

The kick and bass also exist in this area. While the fundamentals of a bass instrument usually occur much lower than the mid-range, the harmonics extend throughout this range, and the transient energy of a kick drum also resides in this area. Therefore, the wrong cut or dynamic movement can also destroy the groove of the music.

Making things more complicated, this is also our phonlea range. If you recall from a previous chapter, our hearing is highly attuned to frequencies between 1 and 5 kHz because this is where the human voice is centred, so it takes little to no effort to hear in this range, but it comes at the expense of hearing the frequencies above and below it.

Many producers often don't realise how much mental effort listening requires. They feel it's a natural process that doesn't require intense focus. Therefore, they usually produce mixes with too much energy centred here and not enough directly above or below it. Indeed, many less experienced producers will fill this range because synthesiser presets and samples are produced within this frequency band. If you ever have the opportunity to visit the trading floor at NAMM, you will experience how overused it is.

NAMM is the most significant trade and professional show held annually in Los Angeles, USA, with an attendance of over forty thousand people. As you walk around the floor, you are bombarded with the sound of synthesisers, guitars, shows, displays, presentations, and, of course, crowds. Everybody is vying for your attention.

Synth manufacturers know trade shows are noisy, and they need potential clients to hear what their latest synth can do, so presets are often designed to sit in the phonlea so they can be heard over the noisy environment. Even sub-bass has exceptional energy in the phonlea because you will not hear a "normal" sub bass timbre over the noise.

This feeds into music production, especially with inexperienced producers. As they select samples, they don't realise that their energy lies in the 1 to 5 kHz range, resulting in a wall of sound with little else occurring directly above or below it. These are all factors we must consider when approaching mastering the mid-range frequencies.

As I mentioned previously, to deal with the midrange, I like to subdivide them into further ranges and examine their effect on music. The subdivision is shown below.

400 – 600 Hz – Low mid – range
600 – 2000 Hz – Mid – range
2000 – 4000 Hz – Upper mid – range
4000 – 6000 Hz – Presence

400–600 Hz Lower Mid-Range

The lower mid-range characterises many sounds because this is where their fundamental frequencies exist. While bass's fundamental frequency will typically be lower than this, a significant portion of its energy will reside here, providing the tone's sonic richness and textures.

This area can be challenging to hear accurately; two-way monitor systems only sometimes represent this area with any degree of accuracy, and because it resides just below the phonlea, it takes some significant listening skills to pick it out and hear what is occurring.

EQ adjustments should have a low Q value and no more than a couple of dB in adjustment. Increasing the band will often increase the bass's tonal presence, adding depth and solidity, but it will also affect the fundamentals of other instruments and can reduce definition. If you increase this band too much, it will often reduce the clarity of higher-frequency elements. Multi-band processing or effects must be used cautiously here, too. I wouldn't recommend placing a band between this area as the filter's phase shift will weaken the bass tone.

600–2000 Hz Mid-Range

This range is formidable to hear because it starts below the phonlea but extends into it. The most difficult is the 600–900 Hz; these frequencies are often considered "boxy", and any EQ reduction will always sound like an improvement because it will add clarity to the higher range.

However, while it will be perceived to add clarity, reducing this area too much will make the music, particularly the bass, sound thin on radio broadcasts and streaming platforms. Moreover, smart speakers, such as Alexa and Apple Homepod, have energy focus in this range, so if removed, the music will appear to lack energy.

Many producers "miss" this range because it is so difficult to hear. There can be a lot of leftover "trash" here, so EQ boosting may bring forward boxiness or a lack of sonic definition. If there are problems here, rather than EQ, I prefer multi-band compression as this can control the transient behaviour, which often controls the boxy nature of this region.

2000–4000 Hz Upper Mid-Range

This is the phonlea, where we are most sensitive to frequencies. Instruments with lower frequency fundamentals exhibit their upper harmonic frequencies in this range, so we must pay attention to the instruments and their clarity of pitch and texture.

If the fundamental frequency is obscured, we must be cautious of cuts; if the fundamental is present, we must be careful of boosts. Altering the balance between the fundamental and its additional harmonics can significantly harm the material, reducing the music's clarity.

Compression rarely serves any purpose in this range as there are few transients; therefore, you must be cautious of what will trigger the compressor. Saturation, however, can add presence to this range, adding a gentle thickening with triodes (if required!) that can add clarity and focus to the music. We must, however, be cautious of creating ear fatigue by over-emphasising this region.

4000 Hz–6000 Hz Presence

The presence range is transparency, adding detail to instruments, particularly speech and hi-hats. Modifications in this area can improve the clarity and detail of vocals and bring hi-hats, acoustic guitars, and leads forward. Exaggerating this range will introduce a brittle sound to the music, but it will lose detail and transparency if reduced too much.

Saturation here often reduces the transparency of the music, and compression should be handled carefully. Like the upper mid-range, we must be cautious of what drives the compressor. Smaller Q values of 0.7 EQ perform better than higher, and I like to use minimal phase in this region due to the colouration it adds. Linear phase can often result in ringing when used in the presence range.

Mid-Range Overall

The mid-range is particularly busy regarding the fundamentals and harmonics of most instruments, including the vocals. Female vocals typically reside from 350 to 17000 Hz, while males tend to sit significantly lower, ranging from 100 to 8000 Hz. So, consider what you apply if you are working on a vocal mix. If processing is too heavy-handed, you can dull the vocals, killing the mix.

You can use a digital, clinical EQ or a gentler analogue EQ. Most resonance occurs in this area, so it will require a linear phase to remove, but any other adjustments typically sound better with a minimal phase EQ. The maximum Q value should be 0.9, as slightly wider movements tend to sound more natural.

We are particularly sensitive to this area, so any changes must be carefully applied. I prefer a Charter Oak PEQ-01 because this is designed to make the mid-range boosts and cuts slightly smaller. I follow this with an API 5500 EQ, as the tone and colour of this EQ are particularly suited to the mid-range frequencies, adding warmth and vibrancy (Figure 15.1).

Note that adjusting the frequencies in the high and lows or the mid-range will impact the balance of the mix, and we must strive to maintain the spectral balance of the music. Removing frequencies in the middle will increase the bass and highs, giving the impression of a better sound because this is what we experience with volume.

If the music appears empty, weak, or lacking energy, this is typically due to a lack of frequency content in the mid-range. Two approaches to repair this are compression, saturation, or both.

Figure 15.1 The API 5500 is precise but adds a welcoming colour, tone, and character to the mid-range.

Gentle compression on the mid-range (as a whole) with a fast attack and slower release will capture the transients and reduce their energy, increasing the signal density of the upper harmonics. This will add more presence and body to the music, but the release must be configured so that compression is not constantly engaged; otherwise, it will distort the material. If the compressor has an auto-release, it would be best to use it.

Alternatively, saturation in the midrange can provide a distortion that gives a track fullness. I prefer second-order harmonic distortion in the midrange, accomplished via triode, but we must ensure that it does not create phase issues or smear the transients. If you smear the mid-range, then the vocals can become unclear.

Saturation or compression may increase the presence, resulting in a brittle sound, but rather than correct this with EQ, I prefer to use a de-esser. It can reduce the brittle effect if set appropriately without phasing the audio.

Employing a stereo widener on the mid-range can also be appropriate, although I will typically limit this to the upper mid-range and above (above 2 kHz). This ensures I miss the fundamentals of the instruments and only push their upper harmonics further into the field, creating more space in the higher elements of the mix. This ensures that if the mix is played in mono, it does not affect the placement of instruments.

Chapter 16
Mastering High-Range Frequencies

High-range frequencies range from 6 to 20 kHz and higher. I say higher because although we can only perceive frequencies from 20Hz to 20 kHz, many argue that sounds above our hearing limitation – in the ultrasonic range – contribute to audio's spatial depth and soundstage.

Some bloggers, journalists, and early research suggest that our organs respond to ultrasonic frequencies, as these have been detected in rainforests. This explains why we feel differently in one. It also explains why monitor speakers extend beyond 20 kHz and why some EQs are designed to work with frequencies higher than our hearing limitations.

I don't feel there is enough scientific evidence to suggest these ultrasonic frequencies contribute to "air or space" in music, and our perception is likely altered by what we read. Similarly, it is unlikely to affect our organs unless expressly targeted with incredibly high resolution. Instead, I'd argue that the experience of actually being present **in** a rainforest would make anyone feel differently.

Ultrasonic frequencies can, however, affect sound due to the nonlinear response when mixed with lower frequencies. A Theremin, for example, sometimes creates an ultrasonic frequency combined with an audible tone at a lower frequency to make its tone.

Furthermore, monitor speakers reach much higher frequencies because extending the system's response reduces piston break-up, ensuring consistency and better sound in lower octaves. The latest Apple Homepod has five tweeters for precise vocal and instrument reproduction. In addition, EQs that extend beyond 20 kHz are not designed because we can hear this high but because they permit a shelf's centre frequency to exist *above* 20 kHz, changing its knee response in the audible range.

DOI: 10.4324/9781032685229-17

Nonetheless, it is important to note that when mastering music, it is not essential to have the high-frequency hearing perception of a bat. While having trained ears, a good monitoring environment, and a knowledgeable approach are necessary; there is little to no musical content above 14 kHz.

Of course, if you remove all content above 14 kHz, air or detail is often lost, but anything above 16 kHz does not significantly affect the music. I've known EDM mastering engineers to roll off frequencies above this range. MP3 compression algorithms do the same, and while some complain that they can hear the algorithm's compression working on the higher frequencies, they're probably reacting to the phase distortion created by the algorithm filters rather than the higher frequency content.

High-frequency waves are short and, therefore, dissipate more readily through air. Due to the short wavelength, high frequencies do not travel as far as low frequencies, so you can't hear them unless you are close to the source. However, while they may not contribute to the vibrations that make us want to dance, frequencies from 6 to 14 kHz create tension in music, helping us distinguish between different instruments and providing clarity in vocals. You only have to consider using a low-pass filter sweep in dance music and the anticipation and energy it creates to understand how higher frequencies add to the tension and excitement of music.

Mastering High Frequencies

Frequencies between 6 and 20 kHz are often known as the brilliance range. We must ensure they are smooth and bright when dealing with this area. It is a fine line between pleasant and unpleasant. The highs in music will appear brittle or jarring if they are too pronounced, making the music unlistenable. However, if this frequency range is too dull, there will be a need for more clarity and air in the music.

The most common problem I experience with mastering are mixes that exhibit too much energy in this range. This is either a result of poor monitoring, hearing loss, or the "smiley" EQ curve. I've spoken about this earlier: as we increase volume, we perceive mid-range to dip in amplitude, emphasising low and high frequencies.

We must be wary when performing any EQ in the higher-frequency range with plugins because we don't want to create EQ cramping. This was discussed in an earlier chapter and occurs when we use a bell EQ curve close to Nyquist. The bell curve will lose symmetry, creating a brittle or unstable cramping sound, whether boosting or cutting.

I recommend using an analogue EQ because there is no Nyquist, and the A/D conversion back into the system will use anti-aliasing filters. If you must use a plugin, I'd recommend using a de-esser, a high-frequency compressor, or a shelving filter.

While a de-esser is designed to reduce sibilance in vocals, it can also help tame the higher frequencies in a master. These are dynamic compressors intended to work within specific frequency ranges. Although some will not extend high enough to control extremely high-frequency energy, they can often work well on the material.

A high-frequency compressor, such as the Sony Oxford Suppressor, is a better alternative. This allows you to tune into the offending frequency range and set the dynamic restriction amount. Compression occurs dynamically whenever the signal exceeds the threshold, restricting the material. Dynamic control often sounds better with higher frequencies than frequency control (Figure 16.1).

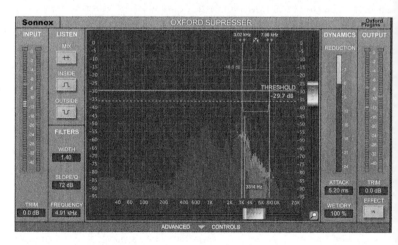

Figure 16.1 Sony Oxford Suppressor is sometimes a preferable approach to EQ for taming high frequencies.

The final approach is to employ an EQ, but I suggest a shelving filter rather than a bell curve. Additionally, I would use a dynamic EQ so that the shelf isn't constant, and the frequency correction only occurs when they exceed a specific threshold.

This is because the higher frequencies add air and space to the soundstage of the mix. When the mix is quiet, with less instrumentation, you want to ensure the filter remains open so the blend can breathe. Only when it becomes energetic can you control higher frequencies because these mask the "air" of the music.

I can't recall ever receiving a master that lacked high frequencies, so I've never had to boost the higher frequencies, but if required, I would use a dynamic shelving EQ to increase them. However, I have often had to focus on the 6–12 kHz range to add clarity to vocals or control resonances from overzealous cymbals, particularly ride cymbals and sometimes open hats.

Although a large amount of vocal content is in the mid-range, it continues into the higher frequencies. We have preconceived expectations with vocals, and although we can affect them in various ways, the higher-frequency content is essential to maintain clarity in the words. The high-end range will suffer when they have been heavily processed, particularly with formant processing.

This can make them sound muddy and undistinguishable, but this may be a deliberate creative decision made by the producer, so always double-check first. I like using a dynamic EQ to cure vocals, ensuring that small boosts only occur when required. This must be a low Q value, typically under an octave (0.7), to ensure I don't pull out resonance. I like to use Fabfilter Pro Q3 for these purposes, although plenty of dynamic EQ plugins are available, and I recommend trying a few demos before settling on your tool of choice (Figure 16.2).

There are hardware versions of dynamic EQs, but these are few and far between. A hardware option I sometimes use is the SSL Bus +2, which has a mastering-grade dynamic EQ. This has a low and high-frequency dynamic range function. The high frequency is a default shelf setting starting at 6 kHz or a bell at 4 kHz. So, although this can be handy, I often refer back to the Q3 if I need to be more precise (Figure 16.3).

Crash cymbals, ride cymbals, and open hi-hats are usually problematic in this range, and there is often resonance or excessive hiss and

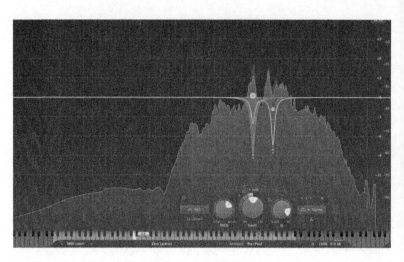

Figure 16.2 Fabfilter Pro Q3 for dynamic EQ.

Figure 16.3 SSL Bus +2 is one of the few hardware dynamic EQs.

brightness from the instrument, usually due to poor tuning. I'll control these with an EQ, usually a linear phase with a high Q (30 +) and approximately 4–6 dB cuts. I'll always use a dynamic EQ with this to ensure it only acts when the resonance exceeds the threshold.

I try to avoid multi-band compression on these higher frequencies due to the phase introduced at the crossover points; it's not a good idea to introduce phase at 6 kHz (the beginning of this brilliance band) because the phase occurs right across the presence, resulting in the instruments losing clarity. Instead, as mentioned, I will use the suppressor plug-in.

I recommend listening closely to this band when employing wideband compression. As you increase the release time, this band is heavily affected, becoming duller with shorter, longer times. This can be useful for controlling an excessive high-end. If, however, the high end is already dull and lacking energy, shorter times may be preferential to maintain some high-frequency content rather than reducing it and attempting to increase it later artificially.

I am cautious about any saturation effects in this band. It can soften harshness on the higher frequencies and compress bright transients to tame them, but if it's a plug-in, it may also introduce aliasing. When applying, you should also listen closely to its side-effects on the midband, as these may lose clarity.

Chapter 17
Mastering Process Step by Step

With all the theories behind mastering discussed, we can now examine how I approach mastering in a more practical setting.

I'm in a position where I do not master my work, so all files I receive from clients are new to my ears; however, if you are mastering music that you produced and mixed, I recommend several days working on something else to ensure you have what I call "clean ears." I understand you'll be excited to master and release it upon the world, but we often get very close to a project; when mastering it, we should be fresh to the audio.

After loading the audio into your DAW or audio editor, I perform an initial listening and assessment of the music. This often involves listening to the file three or four times completely and making notes of anything I hear that I feel needs correcting.

Mastering is a different approach to production. We do not jump in, throw processors on, and twiddle until we reach something we think is right. We must first make a series of judgements and then instantiate the tools to accomplish it. If you jump straight in with tools, you can damage the music while believing you are making it better because changes to the dynamic density of the material or any of the volume and frequency adjustments, even if they're poor, will make the music seem more appealing to your ears.

We can begin by examining my process before I even reach for a processor. Of course, some of these will not apply unless you have received the music from a client, but I will cover the processes regardless.

DOI: 10.4324/9781032685229-18

1. Read the engineer's notes.

    If the audio is delivered from a client, read through any attached production or mix notes. Most professionals do not mix their music and send it to an engineer. All mix engineers will typically include notes about the mix and what they feel may be problematic for the mastering engineer. Always take the time to read these and make notes.

2. Check the sample rate.

    A master should always be delivered the same as it is received unless the client specifically requests a different sample or bit depth. When the file is loaded into your DAW, you should ensure you work at the same sample rate.

    If your DAW is configured to 44.1 kHz and the file is 48 kHz, it can be challenging to notice the difference beyond slight distortion occurring on higher frequencies. Applying your processing without noticing this difference doesn't produce a great master. Ensure the interface, DAW and clock are all set appropriately!

3. Listening level

    On the initial listen, use headphones and set the volume to the level of conversational speech; you mustn't listen too loud at this stage. While it is necessary to feel the music and form an attachment to it, louder invariably sounds better and will affect your judgement; you are not listening to dance around the room to it.

    Headphones will bring out the finer details of the music, which you should concentrate on first. Then, it would be best to listen again through monitors at the conversation level. Listening too loud may push your monitors to their maximum excursion, reducing the fidelity of the music and causing your ears to fatigue quickly.

    While mastering, occasionally increase and decrease the volume to check edits do not negatively affect the music at different volumes. Almost all music sounds better louder, so it is more important that it sounds great at low volumes as well as high.

4. Reference track

    You should have requested a reference track from the client to understand what they're thinking. This isn't to drop in your

DAW and reference; you can use this to see what your client considers to be an appropriate volume level and what they think is the correct spectral balance, and it also forms an idea of what is expected from you.

Listen to the tempo, tonal balance, and dynamics and consider whether these apply to the track for the master. Occasionally, clients have unrealistic expectations, believing their track can sound like a commercial release with some professional mastering when their music is a million miles away from the reference.

Note that mastering is a skill and an art form. Although it is helpful that a client sends a reference track, don't be led by it. A reference track is nothing more than an example. It is not a set prescription that has to be duplicated.

Do not use an EQ clone plugin; these use the reference track and apply the spectral balance, ambience, or macro spectral envelope, and all music is different! Composition, instrument selection, and arrangement influence a track's spectral balance and dynamics.

It is also likely that the reference track is an MP3; remember, these use filters to remove frequencies that it perceives as not audible. All filters add phase distortion, so the MP3 will exhibit some distortion that can make it appear different.

5. Ensure the whole track is present.

We all make mistakes, mainly clients in a rush and DAWs with bugs. When they bounce the audio, it may result in a clip or pop at the start or may miss the beginning. Similarly, they miss off the reverb tail at the song's end, or some delays may be missing.

Listen carefully to the start and end of the song. If it ends in reverb or delays, ensure they are all present. You do not want to deliver a master only to have the client complain that the end is missing – it will always be your fault!

I recommend applying a short fade at the very end of every track. This fade does not affect the music but ensures that there are no clicks or pops when the audio is printed.

6. Are there dynamics to work with?

While many mastering engineers request the file delivery be at -12 dBFS RMS, this is less important than receiving a file with dynamics present. Many amateur mixers follow the YouTube presenter's advice of mixing through a compressor. While this makes their mixes sound better due to increased signal density, it heavily restricts the material's dynamic behaviour.

While we ask for any bus processing to be removed before submission of the file if the client has mixed through a compressor, the mix falls apart when its removed, and so many will leave it on and not mention it. Or if they do remove it, they expect it to sound like it has been through a mix bus compressor after mastering. If the material is lacking in dynamics, you will be extremely limited with processing. In this case, you should talk to the engineer.

7. Check the stereo balance
It would be best to use a goniometer vector scope to monitor the mix to ensure equal stereo balance. Some mixes will lean towards the left or right due to hearing loss, poor wiring, faulty equipment, dodgy plug-ins, or lack of attention. You can typically correct these issues with the vector scope if it has independent volume adjustments or a stereo balance plugin. This imbalance is more common than you may think, which is why many mastering switchers feature independent gain control.

8. Check for mono compatibility
Regardless of the information on the internet, mono compatibility is essential for any mix. How can half a billion smart speaker users be wrong? Alongside using a correlation meter to see if there is a lack of correlation, I recommend playing the mix in mono and comparing the results. Poor mono compatibility will usually result in instruments appearing quieter or phase issues that affect the intelligibility of the music.

The Mastering Process

If all of the above pass your checks, you can approach the process of mastering the track. What follows should not be considered the ultimate guide because all music is different and requires a different approach to ensure you maintain its musicality. We do not apply processing just because we have it, and we should think the opposite by asking if the processing is necessary.

Figure 17.1 LetItMix GainMatch.

All of the techniques I discuss here have been discussed throughout the book, so this should be considered the order in which I approach music and some of the steps I may take.

It is essential that every time you apply any processing, regardless of what it is, you consistently A/B between the processed and the non-processed version to confirm your edits are improving the material and not harming it. Because the processing will likely adjust the volume, and any volume increments will alter our perception of the music, you should also insert a plug-in that compensates for any gain changes.

Numerous plug-ins, such as Meterplugs Perception, Nugen Audio's Mastercheck, and LetitMix GainMatch, can accomplish this. In GainMatch, for example, you place the transmitter plugin *before* the processing chain and the receiver plugin *after* the chain. Regardless of what processing you apply between these, the volume remains consistent, allowing you to judge based on the processing alone rather than volume changes (Figure 17.1).

1. Remove pops, clicks, or crackles.
    We should listen to the audio for any pops, clicks, crackles, or quantisation errors. Tools can remove pops, clicks, and crackles, but I wouldn't recommend them during mastering unless you have no other option because they will affect the rest of the file.

    For example, a click remover will often affect the transients of the material, reducing their impact, and anti-crackle software can remove the aura of reverb, further damaging the mix.

    While quantisation noise is unlikely, I've received the occasional mix where it has been evident. This is usually most noticeable on reverb tails, such as just before the drop when the vocalist performs their last word and reverb decays to silence before the mix drops back in. You can hear the quantisation noise in the reverb due to using a poor effects plug-in.

In all these instances, I would return the mix to the engineer. Any attempts to repair these can cause more harm than good. While we cannot solve quantisation problems, in extreme circumstances, I may attempt to fix pops and clicks but automate these only to occur when the click is present.

2. Control the resonance.

I always listen for resonances in the mix before any other process. These short, sharp, piercing harmonics accompany an instrument or appear when two instruments co-occur. As discussed previously, I would not recommend applying significant boosts to find these or trust an FFT, but rather, listen carefully to the audio to identify them.

Some plug-ins, such as Oeksound Soothe2, are designed to identify resonant frequencies in a mix. This is an automated process that identifies problematic resonances and reduces them dynamically. I've had varying success using it; sometimes, it has worked well, and other times, it has misidentified the resonances and damaged the audio.

I often use a linear phase EQ to minimise phase issues, but it depends on the frequency and the results. Sometimes, the linear phase will introduce ringing artefacts, so I must use a minimal phase. I recommend using a dynamic EQ to address these issues so that minimal processing occurs only when necessary.

3. Adjust clarity.

Clarity may seem like an unusual application for mastering, and generally speaking, it can be. This is something that should have been attained during the mixing process. Still, while listening, if the vocals seem a little far back in the mix or the kick's attack seems ill-defined, I may apply a gentle wide EQ boost of just a few dB to see if I can bring it to where it should be to maintain clarity. Provided these movements are gentle and don't upset the music's spectral balance, they can provide a presence that enhances the music.

4. Maintain spectral balance.

This is sometimes referred to as the total balance or ambience of the music. A spectral imbalance is common in most masters, typically from too much low-end or high-end activity. Correcting this depends on the amount of activity and its cause. Sometimes, a Baxandall EQ can be used, while a multi-band compressor may be preferable other times.

If the mid-band frequencies lack energy, reducing the highs and bass is preferable to boosting the mid-range unless you use a passive EQ, as boosts via active EQs or compression sound more unnatural than cuts. I may also use mid-side processing here if required.

Using a passive EQ to increase the midrange effectively reduces the low and high frequencies to boost the midrange while maintaining a more natural musical sound. This is why many engineers prefer passive EQs for mastering.

5. Control the dynamics.

Once the balance is correct, I'll approach the dynamics. I use compression mostly to add further clarity or increase the density of the music by re-shaping the transients. I may also use it to add some tone.

How this is applied depends entirely on the music, but compression typically follows EQ, not vice versa. If EQ follows compression, the compressor will not control any frequency-based adjustments, which can upset the tonal colouration. Of course, this is a suggestion and not a rule, and it all depends on what works with the music. I may also use mid-side processing here if required.

6. Listen to the silence.

Silence is just as important as the music. Several EDM tracks will drop to silence before a drop or reprise of the music. Unless intentional background noise is present, it should be silent, so ensure it is. Dynamic manipulation on a track may bring up noise to an audible level, so always listen after compression. In one recent project, I had to edit the audio file to remove background noise caused by a hardware synthesiser.

7. Apply Stereo Widening

I'm not a proponent of applying artificial stereo widening with a master. While I know many mastering engineers use it for every mix because it has the wow factor with a client, I only apply it if the mix lacks so much stereo information that it's nearly mono. In this instance, I'll apply it lightly using phase rather than mid-side, for reasons discussed in earlier chapters.

Once the stereo widening has been applied, I'll recheck the mix using a goniometer and a correlation meter. I will also listen in mono to verify that it hasn't degraded the audio or reduced its mono compatibility.

8. Limit the music.

The music can be limited once the mix is balanced in spectral content and dynamics. As discussed in a previous chapter, I will use several limiters rather than set a single unit to stun because it preserves the integrity of the music. Your mileage may vary.

I intend to maintain a PLR value between 7 and 9 to preserve the punch, which is more important than the overall LUFS value. The PSR may occasionally drift into 4 or 5 depending on the density and dynamic activity in the music but provided it doesn't remain low, it gives a balanced master. With most records I've mastered, maintaining this approach results in values ranging from -7 to -11 (I)LUFS on the final master.

9. Add metadata or ISRC codes.

Metadata is information stored in the audio file. On playback, it provides credit information such as the artist, track, release date, album name, additional musicians, and mixing and mastering engineers. The International Standard Recording Code (ISRC) is used to identify the recording, not the work. Generally speaking, different recordings and remixes of the same work should each have their own ISRC. However, if you plan to release records on Spotify, using the same ISRC code means that listeners will be directed to all your songs rather than just one.

The metadata and ISRC can be entered when bouncing the music for final distribution, and most DAWs account for this, permitting you to enter the data as you see fit. Different file formats accept various types of metadata, however. AIFF, FLAC, and MP3 accept detailed metadata, whereas WAV is limited in what data you can enter. While we should always return a file in the same format delivered, I suggest to the client that AIFF is a better format than WAV due to the metadata (Figure 17.2).

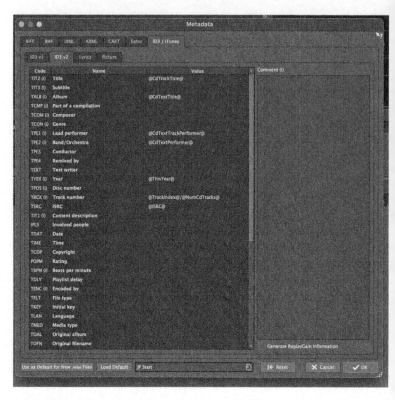

Figure 17.2 The metadata tab in Wavelab.

Chapter 18
Practical Application

With all the theories behind mastering discussed, I thought it best to end the book with a real-world practical example of how I approach a master. For this example, I will use "Every Beat Of My Heart" by Nicky Holloway.

Nicky is an English DJ and record producer who, along with Paul Oakenfold, Johnny Walker, and Danny Rampling, was one of the four DJs responsible for bringing house music to the United Kingdom in 1987. I've been working with Nicky for a few years on several of his albums, and he kindly permitted me to use one of the many tracks I mastered for him as an example.

Since many readers still need to develop significant aural memory, we will work on this example with over 62 bars of the music. My approach is the same throughout the track, but using a smaller section will make it easier for you to hear the changes I implement. You can listen to the demo at www.altaracademy.com

We should start by listening to **Every_Beat_1**; you can listen to it on the website or download the pack with all the files enclosed. I recommend downloading the package and placing them all in your DAW on separate channels so you can A/B between them.

So that our listening is not affected by volume, I have processed all of the files to -24 (I)LUFS, so the volume of each example is generally the same. Any differences we hear are solely from the processing I've applied and not from a volume change.

Since we regularly converse with Nicky, no notes existed beyond instructions to master the track. We're not using reference tracks, as Nicky doesn't like to supply them, as he has his sound: commercial/

DOI: 10.4324/9781032685229-19

classic house music. The file's sample rate is 44.1 kHz, and the bit rate is 24-bit. You can hear (or see) from the waveform of **Every_Beat_1** that there is plenty of dynamic energy in the music by looking at the crest factor between the peak and RMS value. The amplitude is approximately -9 dBFS RMS.

Throughout this practical example, I will use a mix of hardware and software; this is how I work. However, all of the hardware processors I use can be replaced with digital plugins, whether these are software emulations of the hardware or general plug-ins designed to perform the same function.

Every_Beat_1 – Listening

This is the original supplied mix. Listening back, the mix is mono-compatible, but I did notice that the mix leans ever so slightly to the left. This could be due to a faulty plug-in or incorrect setting, but we can correct this using the Goniometer, as it permits us to adjust the left/right amplitude.

There are no pops and clicks in the music but several resonant frequencies. These were not identified by automated software such as Oeksounds Soothe2 but are nonetheless present.

1. The word "heart" is unstable and slightly distorted. The distortion is intentional, but after speaking with Nicky, the instability is from the source, so it can't be repaired and will have to form a part of the record's character.
2. If you listen closely to the vocal "With every little beat of my heart," the "heart" also exhibits a slight whistle when the vocalist/talent performs. This occurs around 3.2 kHz.
3. Each snare hit has a resonance to its strike; the initial transient exhibits some resonance that whistles on every strike, occurring around 4.5 kHz.
4. The snare sounds boxy in the middle, creating a hollow, loose texture.
5. There is resonance occurring on an instrument, which becomes most prominent behind the vocalist when she sings "beat", "of", and "my". I don't believe this is the vocal, but an instrument behind it occurs at approximately 1.2 kHz.

6. Another resonance occurs at approximately 900 Hz, causing a hollow whistle in the midrange.
7. There is a resonance at 600 Hz, causing a lower-frequency hollow inaccuracy.
8. There is a slight problem in the low mid-range at 160 Hz, which pronounces the bass strike, adding a boxy character to the bass line.
9. The kick lacks the energy and punch we would expect from the genre.
10. The bass is too light and needs the top-end presence.
11. The piano exhibits a boxy nature in the low mids and lacks presence in the high mids.
12. The mix lacks air, and it sounds flat at higher frequencies.

It's important to note that I won't attempt to repair one or all of these with a singular processor or plug-in. Many producers throw plug-ins onto a mix (or master) and set everything to stun to repair a problem. This is where knowing your tools is essential.

I know that I cannot, for example, fix the snare with a single tool. Instead, it will take several carefully adjusted processors, each affecting a part of the snare and contributing to its overall sound. However, as this is a complete mix, I must repair everything else simultaneously, carefully approaching the processing individually and ensuring that as I repair the snare, I also repair the bass and the vocals without causing damage to any other instrumentation.

This is the process of mastering. We hear problems and use several processors to eventually bring everything under control piece by piece rather than relying on one processor to treat one issue and then another to treat another problem. This is why I believe AI cannot yet replace a mastering engineer; it can't identify these problems and can only impose the spectral and dynamic balance onto music.

Every_Beat_2 – Pro Q3 EQ

I approached these resonances using Pro-Q3 set to a linear phase, using a Q value of approximately 30 and applying roughly 3 to 5 dB cuts to the material. If you listen carefully to Every_Beat_2, you can hear how the vocal sounds more relaxed and less "tinny", while the bass and snare no longer sound as boxy. These differences are subtle, but we must approach these with various tools to repair them, and you must take the time to A/B between the two files until you can identify them.

You cannot boost frequencies to find problems because any frequency boosts will sound like a problem. We have to listen to the mix carefully, using both headphones and monitors, to source potential resonance problems with the mix.

Every_Beat_3 – Charter Oak PEQ 1 & API 5500

I ran the mix through the Charter Oak PEQ 1. This EQ can add clarity and warmth to signals. I applied a slight boost of 1dB at 2 kHz to bring out the vocals and the very top of the snare drum, alongside an increase of 1 dB at 8 kHz to add some air to the music. I also applied a slight 1 dB boost at 800 Hz to add body to the mid of the bass and the snare. It is essential to always A/B any edits and listen beyond what you are repairing to see what else could be changing in the mix.

Using the API 5500, I added a 0.5 dB increase at 15 kHz, a hi-mid cut of 1 dB at 3 kHz, and a low-mid boost of 0.5 dB at 240 Hz. By cutting at 1 dB, I prevented the resonance from returning in the vocals, and the 15 kHz introduced the highs of the hi-hats, brightening up the very top of the mix.

The API has a specific character that will add a forward mid-presence when applied across a mix, even when no processing occurs. This, alongside the boost at 15 kHz, adds to the mid-range energy, bulking up the piano and vocals and adding presence and air around the hi-hats.

Every_Beat_4 – The Drawmer 76

I noted that some EQ movements introduce a slight resonance in the piano and upper-mid area. The mix required EQ to add clarity and presence to the mid and upper mid-range; otherwise, it wouldn't translate appropriately on systems, but I need to control any resonance that may occur.

I also noted that the shakers sitting behind the snare sounded flat. I wanted to pull these out to add more clarity to the upper midbands. The best way to accomplish this is via the Drawmer 76. I can spread the high bands out slightly, revealing the shakers, but if the cross-over point occurred close to the piano, the filter phase could be used to control resonances occurring there.

Every_Beat_5 – SPL PassEQ

The SPL PassEQ is a passive EQ that allows for more substantial changes without affecting the mix too heavily. I used this to add a slight bass increase to the signal, cutting 2 dB at 30 Hz but then boosting 3 dB at 54 Hz. This is a typical action for a passive EQ, as the cut and boost affect one another, creating a smoother increase in the bass frequencies.

I added a 2 dB boost at 1k3 (1.3 kHz) with a 1.5 dB cut at 1 kHz. This smoothed the vocal, upper bass, and snare, which had sounded slightly "peaky" after the previous EQ adjustments.

Every_Beat_6 – SPL Iron Mastering Compressor

I used the mastering compressor to add some glue, particularly to the lower frequencies of the mix. A slower attack allows the kick to pull through (second position on Germanium 2mf). Then, by adjusting the release, I set it long enough that the mix didn't pump (as pumping wouldn't suit this genre) but not too long that it removed the higher-frequency air I added (third position).

I didn't use Air Bass or tape roll-off as I felt it would add too many lows or steal the highs from the mix.

The Tube Bias was set to medium to add more tube sound to the compression. Adding a vintage tube sound to the music, which complements the genre, was more appropriate. If you listen closely and A/B between 5 and 6, you can hear how the kick develops a more resounding, weighty "punch" while the intensity of the bass warms up and sits forward, adding a thickness to the low end, which enhances its sound and suits the genre. I only applied 1 dB of gain reduction to the mix.

Every_Beat_7 – Looptrotter Emperor

The mix would benefit from some very gentle saturation. This enriches the upper-mid frequencies, which sound flat and affect the overall spectral balance. The harmonic saturation will also enhance the snare and bass frequencies while acting as a FET limiter, slightly increasing all transients' punch and presence. I applied the Looptrotter lightly so that it registered no more than 3 dB gain reduction.

Every_Beat_8 – BetterMaker Mastering Limiter

The final analogue stage was the mastering limiter; I prefer using a series of analogue limiters to crushing the signal with a single digital limiter at the final stage. I used the analogue limiter to apply 4 dB of gain reduction at the loudest areas of the music, with the output set to -1 dB for printing back into the DAW.

I added a small amount of third-order harmonic distortion to everything occurring below 230 Hz to vibrate the lower frequencies of the mix. I added some second-order harmonic distortion to frequencies above 1 kHz to make the top of the mix sound more present.

Once the track was finished, I printed it back into the DAW and used the McDSP limiter, followed by the Pro L2 limiter, to raise the volume. I mastered the track to 9.2 PLR, resulting in a LUFS value of -10.4. If I pushed the limiters any harder than this, you could hear the track begin to sound restricted, which will not suit this particular genre of music.

Ultimately, I hope this chapter and its audio examples have shown that many movements in mastering are generally always very subtle. We envision the goal and work towards it, using one processor at a time, knowing how each will affect the other and their effects on the mix.

Stacking processors, each accomplishing a small part, results in not throwing a single processor across the bus and setting it to stun.

This is why mastering is an art form. It does not rely on guesswork. It depends on understanding your tools, their accomplishments, and how they will interact. We make a decision, and then we execute it. If you jump in and make it up as you go along, you're setting yourself up for failure.

Chapter 19
Delivery Formats

I suspect that some readers are doing so simply for an insight into how mastering is performed. Some will want to send their music to a professional mastering engineer rather than approach it themselves. Therefore, the best way to end this book is to include a chapter providing a producer's perspective.

Therefore, I asked Rick Snoman, an experienced mix engineer, how he prepares a mix for mastering. Rick has worked on and mixed tracks for many labels, including Warner, Sony, ToolRoom, Spinnin, Anjuna, Blanco Y Negro, and Mammas Milk, to name just a few.

I'm fortunate to have the opportunity to master many of the mixes Rick works on. When I receive a track from him, I know it'll be submitted in the correct format, have an excellent dynamic range to work with, and will not contain any problems. I don't tell him, but I still check because mastering is the final quality check.

Regardless, since Rick knows how to deliver a mix to a mastering engineer, he will take you through how to prepare for Mastering a track by yourself or your mastering engineer.

Ricks Comments: First, I think it's important to state that there are no industry standards for providing a mix to a mastering engineer, and there are no standard checklists. If you speak or email the mastering house, they will (or should) inform you how they expect the masters to be delivered, and they will supply you with a checklist of how that mastering engineer needs your file.

Many requests are to ensure you maintain some dynamics, that the sample rate and bit depth are sufficient, and there is no processing that may damage the file before they receive it. However, while you are

DOI: 10.4324/9781032685229-20

provided with a checklist, it's surprising how many submissions we receive that have misinterpreted the request or delivered the file with mistakes. Therefore, what follows isn't to suggest what you should be asked for; it's to explain why we ask for what we do and some common mistakes made when submitting files.

Talk to Your Mastering Engineer

After finding an engineer, email them and ask who they have worked with, what their experience is, and what equipment they use. Do some research, but I don't advise asking a professional for a "demo" of their work – they're usually sat in a half-million-pound mastering studio for a good reason.

The price for mastering can range from £15 to £120, and while the latter may seem expensive to some, buy cheap, buy twice. If you are unwilling to invest in your music, you shouldn't be surprised when the record labels and the public aren't either. While it may sound great, we've already heard the presets, splice samples, poor mixing, and terrible mastering a thousand times this past month. Professionals care about their music and how the public receives it; amateurs only care about themselves and their egos.

Do You Need Apple Certification?

A select number of mastering engineers are on the Apple-approved program, ensuring they deliver your master's in Apple-certified formats. When your music is submitted to Apple, they will use the email supplied by your mastering engineer to confirm the engineer is Apple-approved. This will often place your music higher on the Apple music playlists than non-apple approved masters and accompany the approved logo.

WAV or AIFF

Most mastering houses will request either WAV or AIFF files. These are the most popular PC and Apple Mac formats and offer an uncompressed, full-spectrum resolution we can process further. Never send any compressed media; we have received MP3 files for mastering.

Bit Depth

The bit depth is the amplitude resolution, so it must be as high as possible. 24-bit should be considered the lowest resolution to supply. Even if the track is to be mastered for CD or vinyl, you should still deliver it at the highest depth.

That said, never upscale or downscale the bit depth for delivery, as this can add unwanted artefacts. Instead, deliver the file at the bit depth you have been working at. This could be 32-bit or 24-bit, although remember that the mastering house will provide the format exactly as you did. Therefore, if you deliver a 32-bit depth file, you'll receive that depth back unless you specifically request it be at 24-bit.

We recommend delivering at 24-bit because this provides a high amplitude, reducing the possibility of quantisation and also ensures you can give the master directly to the label.

Sample Rate

Like bit depth, the rate at which you supply the file will be the rate at which it is delivered. Do not up-sample, and send the file as is. Many engineers work at 48 kHz because this is the same rate broadcasters use, making transferring files easy. However, there is nothing wrong with working at 44.1, 88.2, 96, or 192 kHz, but unless you specifically request a different sample rate on delivery, you'll receive what you submit.

Remove All Processing from Your Mix Bus

You should remove any processing from the 2-bus, including compressors, saturators, EQ, and limiters. This highlights one of the problems with "mixing through a compressor." While many presenters suggest it will make your mix sound better, the minute it's removed, the entire balance of the mix will change. Mastering engineers ask that all these processors be removed because they will affect *their* processing.

For example, multiple instruments running through any non-linear processor will introduce side bands. While this is unavoidable, the quality and extent of this side-band information will determine how the mix sounds. Using a cheap plug-in to compress or saturate the mix may sound pleasing to your ears, but it will not sound better than the hardware equivalent. Everything you apply on a mix bus will damage the material, and if you've ruined the sound, a mastering engineer cannot repair it.

Maintain Dynamic Range

Mastering engineers typically ask for approximately 6 dB of headroom above the mix to give them room to work; however, they are asking for some *dynamic* headroom. You can submit a mix with 6 dB of headroom but no dynamic range, giving the engineer nothing to work with.

They are more interested in a higher crest factor, enabling them to apply processing while ensuring they maintain some dynamics for streaming. You can supply a mix that hits -1 dBFS if you want, but provided it has dynamics; they can work with it.

Turn OFF Any Normalising Functions

Many DAWs will normalise a file as they export, essentially increasing the amplitude of your music to 0 dBFS when exporting. While it does not change the dynamics, the high amplitude may exceed the peak value on D/A conversion before we can even work on the file.

Ensure the Start and End of the File Are Correct

I've lost count of the number of masters received that exhibit a click at the start of the track due to the DAW misbehaving or files that do not end properly. You will receive the same length of the file you submit, so if you accidentally bounce another 4 bars of silence at the end, that is what you will receive back.

Mastering engineers are not mind-readers; an echo that stops suddenly, reverb that doesn't decay away fully, noise, or silence at the end of a file are left as is. As far as they know, that is how *you* want the file because this is how you submitted it. If you require a fade-out or fade-in, you should request it.

Provide References ISRC and Metadata

You should provide a couple of example tracks you love that you feel are in the ballpark of your music. The engineer will not insert these into the DAW as a reference (or at least we would hope not), but they can be used to determine what spectral balance you feel your music should exhibit.

If you want ISRC or metadata included in the final delivery format, you should create a text document containing the metadata and input it before the final master is exported to delivery format.

Inform the Engineer of the Intended Delivery Platforms

You should include a text document noting the delivery platforms on which you expect the music to be played. For example, a track will be approached differently if it is only for streaming than for streaming *and* club playback or streaming, club *and* broadcast. These are essential targets, letting the engineer know how much wiggle room they have for the master.

This is especially important if you aim for vinyl, as preparing the medium requires a very different process for a cutting engineer.

Listen to Your Mix Before Sending

After bouncing the music for delivery, wait a few days and then listen to the mix. When listening, make sure it begins correctly, all the instruments are present, there is no distortion or unwanted problems, and the mix plays through until the end and stops when you expect it to.

Index